THE BUSY ENTREPRENEUR'S GUIDE TO DIGITAL MARKETING

EFFECTIVE SEO, SOCIAL MEDIA, AND PAID AD STRATEGIES TO BOOST ONLINE VISIBILITY, ATTRACT CUSTOMERS, AND SCALE YOUR LOCAL BUSINESS

RHOADES CONSULTING GROUP

Copyright © 2024 by Rhoades Consulting Group

All rights reserved.

No portion of this book may be reproduced in any form without written permission from the publisher or author, except as permitted by U.S. copyright law.

This publication is designed to provide accurate and authoritative information in regard to the subject matter covered. It is sold with the understanding that neither the author nor the publisher is engaged in rendering legal, investment, accounting or other professional services. While the publisher and author have used their best efforts in preparing this book, they make no representations or warranties with respect to the accuracy or completeness of the contents of this book and specifically disclaim any implied warranties of merchantability or fitness for a particular purpose. No warranty may be created or extended by sales representatives or written sales materials. The advice and strategies contained herein may not be suitable for your situation. You should consult with a professional when appropriate. Neither the publisher nor the author shall be liable for any loss of profit or any other commercial damages, including but not limited to special, incidental, consequential, personal, or other damages.

Book Cover by Rhoades Consulting Group

Illustrations by Rhoades Consulting Group

First edition 2024

Contents

Introduction	1
1. Understanding the Marketing Landscape Before Diving Into Digital	5
2. Digital Marketing 101	21
3. Knowing Who The F**k You Are	45
4. Building Your Brand Online	58
5. Winning Strategies for Social Media	84
6. Paid Advertising Essentials	105
7. SEO for the Local Market	130
8. Email Marketing Mastery	149
9. Staying Ahead of Digital Marketing Trends	163
10. Conclusion	169
References	175

Introduction

Every day, the digital marketing landscape gets a little tougher and more complex, especially for you, the small, local business owner. You've mastered your craft and built a business from the ground up, but when it comes to digital marketing, it feels like you're trying to climb a mountain in flip-flops.

That stops here.

This book is your map, your guide, and your mentor in navigating the overwhelming world of digital marketing. If you're willing to learn, experiment, and fail a few times along the way, you'll come away with a bullet-proof guide to growing engagement, sales, and revenue.

I can say this because I've invested in the traditional educational route - I have a masters in integrated marketing and communication from Purdue University - and by working with dozens of small business owners I've gotten the hands-on experience of helping people implement this exact plan into their business and reap the rewards. Plus, everything I've written about in this book I've done for my own businesses.

That whole part about failing a few times? Yeah, I've done that too. This has allowed me to bring you the philosophy and the executables while cutting out the fluff so you can get right to work.

Over the years, I've helped small service-based businesses like yours not just survive but thrive, increasing their revenue by implementing practical, effective digital marketing tactics. My approach is simple: forget the fluff; let's get to the stuff that works.

This book is about cutting through the complexity and giving you the knowledge and tools to take control of your digital marketing. You'll learn how to effectively use social media, navigate paid online advertising, and optimize your website for search engines (SEO). More importantly, you'll learn how these strategies can drastically impact your business growth in today's digital age.

I'm not here to lecture you with highbrow marketing theory. Instead, this book promises you 20% theory - so you have a strong foundation - and 80% actionable guide - so you can actually get shit done. It's crafted for small business owners like you who have no time to sift through endless trends and complicated jargon. You need clear, concise, and actionable guidance that you can apply immediately.

Expect this book to be straightforward, blunt, and, yes, even a bit sarcastic at times. Think of it as the tough love no one else will give you. I'm here to deliver the hard truths about digital marketing, to make these complex concepts accessible and maybe, just maybe, a bit more enjoyable to learn.

We'll cover everything from the basics of building a digital marketing strategy to hands-on tactics for maximizing your online presence. Each section of the book is packed with step-by-step guides, practical examples, and real-life case studies to show you exactly how to apply what you're learning.

You're the backbone of this economy—a small business owner, a skilled tradesperson motivated by the drive to grow your business and provide a comfortable life for your family. This book is for you. It's tailored to speak directly to your challenges and aspirations because I've faced those same challenges and pursued similar aspirations. After reading this book and implementing what you learn, you'll no longer need to rely on marketing gurus or fancy ad agencies. Once you take the time to gain this skill set, you can still choose to outsource your business's marketing efforts. But at that point, you're in control and no longer at the mercy of someone else calling shots or pulling strings in your business.

So, dive into this book ready to absorb, implement, and revolutionize your digital marketing strategy. By the end, you won't just understand the digital marketing landscape; you'll be equipped to conquer it and achieve market domination.

If you want to take it a step further, I've also put together a follow-along guide that you can download for free. This guide will help you implement what you learn throughout this book, and if done correctly, you'll have your full-scope digital marketing strategy in-hand. You can snag that workbook at jrhoadesconsultinggroup.com/digitalmarketingworkbook.

Let's get started.

1

Understanding the Marketing Landscape Before Diving Into Digital

Did you know that the average small business owner thinks about marketing 13 times a day? Not because they want to but because they feel they have to. Between running your business, managing your team, and trying to carve out a little time for family, you're also expected to be a marketing guru. It's like being told you need to fly a plane without ever taking a flying lesson. That's where this guide comes in. It's here to show you that marketing isn't just for the "experts" but is something you can master even with the limited time and budget constraints that come with running a small business.

My goal for you at the end of this book is not just to understand how all of the pieces of a marketing strategy can come together to produce results but to become a marketing expert in your own right. I want you to be able to take a look at your business and determine what tactics and pieces are going to work best for you to reach your goals. But to get there, you have to start building a skill set and learn to trust your decision-making when it comes to marketing.

Unfortunately, most small business owners have a limiting belief that they cannot be as good at marketing as they are at their trade. Perhaps that's because it's been portrayed as something only an expert can do well or because the marketing landscape changes so quickly. However, after working with so many small business owners, I've learned that the true reason is they don't want the responsibility of controlling their marketing, and it's easier to blame an ad agency or marketing company for poor results rather than learn to master this new skill and potentially fail at it.

Remember that part where I told you I'd give you some tough love? Well, here it is. This book will ask you to do things you've likely never done before in pursuit of better marketing, so check your ego at the door and approach this information with an open mind and a willingness to put time and effort into what is being asked.

A solid marketing strategy isn't something only the man behind the curtain can do for you; it is absolutely something you can learn and execute on your own. You have to know what to look at, what's available to you, and how to determine if it's all working. This chapter will lay the groundwork for building a robust and well-rounded marketing strategy. Don't worry; we'll get to the specifics of digital tactics, but the reality is that you need this foundation first for any of the digital stuff to work. With this information under your belt, you can be confident that you'll make intelligent, informed interactions with your market.

1.1 What Does 'Marketing' Even Mean?

Somewhere along the lines in our society, maybe with the come-up of the ad men in the 1950s or even the show Mad Men in the 2010s, a common misunderstanding of the marketing profession has been developed and adopted. Marketers are magicians.

These are the guys who know how to spin. The ones who can sell sand at the beach. The guys who turn products into brands and brands into piles of money.

Not only is this an ass-backward perception of the profession, but like I've said before, it's a limiting belief keeping you from being a master of marketing yourself.

Let me start and end here - marketing is how everything in a business comes together to interact with its marketplace.

That's it.

These interactions can include getting people to recognize your product or service, getting people to act and actually purchase it, and getting people to rave about and recommend it to others.

It goes without saying that those interactions can also do the exact opposite, but I'd prefer to stay focused on the possibilities that marketing can offer.

It is important to understand that those interactions happen along a continuum of consciousness. We see anywhere between four thousand and ten thousand ads per day, either via social media, billboards, magazines, or you name it. We can't—and won't—consciously interact with all of these advertisements, but our brain will log them somewhere in the depths of our minds.

Ever start singing the jingle to a commercial or be able to describe the colors and logo of a brand but not be able to name it? Well, if you have enough of these subconscious interactions, you'll start to recall parts of advertisements you see or hear. Over time, when you need to actually use this information, your brain will reach back into its file cabinets and pull out these fragments to create a whole thought. Or at least whole enough for you to recall the name of the service or business that got those fragments stuck there in the first place. These are passive interactions on one side of the continuum.

On the other end of the continuum are the interactions that require effort and personal contact. Do you have a favorite checkout person at your local grocery store because they actually bag your groceries 'correctly'? Do you like your barber because they always ask about your kids? Do you like your dentist because they still let you pull a toy out of the basket even though you're in your thirties? These seemingly insignificant interactions are also marketing. We like it when people make us feel good, heard, or worthwhile. And though this sounds cheesy, you can *purposefully* create these feelings with your prospects or clients.

Every interaction your business has in the market affects how people come to know and think of your brand. You want to control as much of this perception as possible or, at the very least, be aware of it.

Take the time to get really clear on the customer experience from the time a prospect is just a tiny glimmer out in the marketplace to the time they are your paying client giving you a Rolodex of referrals. Do this well, and you will have massive control over your marketing.

Let's do a quick self-evaluation at this point. Ask yourself the following questions:

- In what ways are you and your employees marketing your business?

- What do you think the public's perception of your brand is?

- Where can you make the most improvements?

Understanding that everything your business and employees put into the market is the foundational principle of marketing. Look at every interaction and ask yourself or your team how you can improve it. If there are some things you can implement now, great, do it. Having better interactions and processes now will better your brand reputation and make paid marketing more efficient, too.

Why Marketing Matters Now More Than Ever

In today's digital world, your online presence can be just as important as your physical storefront. The evolution of marketing has shifted significantly with the advent of the internet, social media, and mobile technologies. It's no longer enough to just be the best tradesman in town.

If people can't find you online, or if they do and your digital presence doesn't reflect the quality of your services, you're missing out on a significant chunk of potential business. Digital marketing opens up a new realm of opportunities to connect with customers, build relationships, and grow your business in ways that were not possible before.

In essence, good marketing isn't about mastering complex algorithms or decoding dense textbooks. It's about seeing the value in every handshake, every business card exchange, every customer call, and every social media post. These elements are the building blocks of sound marketing strategy, and they are all actions you are already doing. Now, let's refine them and amplify your business in the digital marketplace.

1.2 The Power of a Full-Scope Marketing Strategy

In the bustling marketplace where your small business lives, understanding that your market is not a static entity but a dynamic, ever-changing beast can significantly alter your approach to marketing. It's a realm where people's needs, preferences, and behaviors shift often subtly, sometimes dramatically. Engaging successfully with such a market requires flexibility and a keen sense of where and when your message will be most effective.

Consider the local chiropractor who offers free consultations for finishers of the upcoming Tough Mudder—by aligning their services with the immediate needs and context of their customers, they not only boost sales but also enhance their reputation as a responsive and customer-centric business. This responsiveness to the market's dynamics is crucial and can significantly ramp up your business's chances of success.

Now, let's talk about a core principle of advertising awareness: the Rule of 7s. In essence, a potential customer needs to encounter your brand at least seven times before they make a purchase decision. This doesn't mean you blast the same ad seven times over a single channel. Instead, think of it as spreading out these interactions across different platforms and mediums—your business's Facebook post one day, a flyer in a local bookstore the next, a mention in a community newsletter later in the week, and so on. This strategy ensures that your business stays top-of-mind without overwhelming potential customers with repetitive messages. It's about achieving a balance that keeps your business visible and engaging without becoming a nuisance.

Furthermore, in the digital age, every penny counts, especially for small businesses operating on shoestring budgets. It's a common misconception that effective marketing requires big bucks. Yes, paid advertising plays a crucial role, but it's not the be-all and end-all of marketing. In fact, a mix of paid and free marketing content can often yield the best results. Take, for example, a local hardware store that uses paid Facebook ads to promote a seasonal sale and complements it with regular, free DIY tips on their blog and social media. This approach draws in customers looking for deals and builds a loyal following that values the store's expertise and regular content updates. By balancing the scales between paid and free content, you create a versatile marketing strategy that maximizes impact while controlling costs.

Lastly, don't underestimate the power of relationship-based marketing methods in your marketing efforts. Simple actions like asking satisfied customers for referrals, engaging with your community through local events, or encouraging word-of-mouth by providing exceptional service can be incredibly effective. These efforts require minimal to no financial investment but can lead to substantial returns. For instance, a local landscaper who sponsors a little league team and gets his business name on the team's jerseys. This not only demonstrates his community involvement but also keeps his business name circulating among local parents, potential customers who might need his services. Such strategies harness the natural interactions and goodwill of everyday business activities, turning them into powerful marketing tools.

In conclusion, a full-scope marketing strategy isn't just about casting the widest net—it's about casting the smartest net. By understanding the dynamic nature of your market, balancing paid and free content, and capitalizing on straightforward, cost-effective marketing methods, your small business can not only survive but thrive in today's competitive landscape.

1.3 Things To Know About Your Business Before You Go To Market

When you're steering the ship of a small business, particularly in a competitive digital market, knowing precisely who you are and what your business stands for isn't just helpful—it's crucial for survival. Let's put it bluntly: the landscape is littered with the husks of businesses that launched into competitive waters without a clear sense of identity or purpose. They failed not necessarily due to a lack of effort or resources but because they lacked a clear definition of success and a roadmap to get there. Understanding who you are, the ethos of your business, and what you aim to achieve forms the bedrock upon which all successful marketing strategies are built.

Think about it this way: if you don't know where you're going, how will you know when you've arrived? Or, more critically, how will you know which path to take or whether you're on the right track? This isn't just about setting goals but about defining what success genuinely means to you and your business. Is it financial stability? Market domination? Customer satisfaction? Likely, it's a blend, but each business will weigh these differently. This clarity isn't just beneficial—it's a necessity. It informs every decision, every campaign, and every customer interaction. Without it, efforts can become disjointed, and resources may be wasted on initiatives that don't align with your ultimate objectives.

Moreover, the essence of who you are as the leader—the CEO of your venture—sets the tone for your entire business. Your beliefs, your ethics, and your vision trickle down to every aspect of operations, from customer service to your marketing messages. For instance, if you value transparency, this should be evident in your marketing content, revealing the real people behind the services and the honesty in pricing or business practices. This authenticity resonates well in today's market, where consumers are not just buying a product or service but buying into what a brand stands for.

Knowing your business also means setting standards for how every team member represents your brand. It's about crafting a company culture that every employee embodies. If your business prides itself on innovation, every team member should be empowered to suggest new ideas. If quality is your cornerstone, meticulousness should be a non-negotiable trait in your staff. This internal clarity and consistency in who you are and what you represent ensures that your business presents a unified front to the world, making your marketing efforts more straightforward, more authentic, and more impactful.

Lastly, let's talk about the mindset with which you approach marketing—or any area of your business, for that matter. Entering the market with a timid approach does more harm than good. If you're not fully committed to implementing your strategies, you're not just standing still; you're moving backward, especially in the digital age where consumer behaviors and technologies evolve swiftly.

Adopting a bold, all-in approach to both building a business and mastering your marketing isn't just advisable; it's a necessity.

This doesn't mean recklessly spending on every marketing trend. Instead, it's about wholeheartedly committing to the strategies you've decided on based on who you are and what you aim to achieve. It's diving deep into the initiatives that align with your business identity and goals, ensuring every dollar and every hour spent moves you closer to your definition of success.

Understanding these foundational aspects of your business before you enter the market can dramatically alter your trajectory. Align your resources, your team, and your strategies with a clear vision of success to ensure that every step taken is a step toward that ultimate goal. It's not just about doing business; it's about doing your business your way, with clarity and purpose at the forefront of every decision.

1.4 The Journey From Market To Customer

Understanding your customer's journey, from first hearing about your business to becoming a loyal advocate, is crucial. It's like tracking the path someone takes through a complex maze; every turn and every decision they make is influenced by how well you've laid out the path for them. From the moment they first hear about your business—maybe through a friend, an online ad, or a social media post—to the moment they decide not just to purchase but to return and even recommend your services, each step is critical.

The first step in this journey is awareness. Are people even aware that your business exists? Think about how often you've discovered a business only because you saw a sign or an online review. That's awareness. It's your job to make sure that when potential customers need your service, your name pops up where they can see it. This could be through search engine results, social media platforms, or even community bulletin boards. Once they know you exist, you've got to pique their interest enough that they want to learn more. This is where they start digging deeper, visiting your website, reading your posts, or checking out your reviews.

Next comes consideration. Now, they're comparing you to your competitors. They're asking, "Why should I choose this business?" Here, your value propositions need to be clear. It could be your unbeatable prices, your superior craftsmanship, or your excellent customer service. Whatever it is, it has to shine through every piece of content they see. The way you respond to reviews, the user-friendliness of your website, and the clarity of your services or products list are all elements that help potential customers make the decision to choose you.

Then, we arrive at the decision stage. They've chosen you, and they're ready to take the plunge. How easy is it for them to take that final step? Can they schedule an appointment easily through your website? Is your contact information front and center? Minimizing friction here is key. A complicated check-out process or hard-to-find contact details can turn a sure thing into a lost opportunity.

Finally, there's loyalty. They've used your service or bought your product. But will they come back? Will they tell their friends? This stage depends heavily on their experience, not just with what you sell but also with all their interactions with your business. Follow-up emails, customer satisfaction surveys, and loyalty discounts—can all help turn a one-time buyer into a long-term advocate.

Now, crafting content that guides a potential customer through this journey doesn't have to drain your wallet. Creative content on a budget might sound like a tall order, but it's entirely doable with a bit of ingenuity. For instance, instead of hiring a pricey professional, why not create simple how-to videos with your smartphone? Show your expertise by demonstrating what you do, offering advice, or sharing insider tips. These videos not only enhance your credibility but also boost your online presence, and they cost next to nothing to produce. Similarly, engaging posts on social media, helpful blog articles, or even eye-catching infographics can be created using free or low-cost online tools. The idea is to provide value that attracts people to your business, making them want to learn more and eventually convert.

Tracking spending and measuring the return on investment (ROI) are equally critical, especially when you're working with a limited budget. It's about ensuring that every dollar you spend on marketing brings value to your business. Start by setting clear objectives for what you want each campaign to achieve, be it more website visits, more phone calls, or more store visits. Use tools like Google Analytics to track how people are finding your website and what they're doing once they get there. Social media platforms offer insights that tell you how many people see and interact with your posts. And don't forget offline methods—ask customers how they heard about you to gauge which of your marketing efforts are working best. Adjust your spending based on what's bringing in the most business. This approach ensures you're not just throwing money out the window but investing it in ways that contribute directly to your business growth.

By understanding and enhancing each step of your customer's journey and being smart about your content creation and budget, you can build a marketing strategy that attracts customers and turns them into long-term patrons of your business. This strategic approach ensures that your marketing efforts create real, measurable results, allowing you to grow your business sustainably, even in a competitive market.

2

Digital Marketing 101

Imagine you're out fishing. You've got your line cast in what you hope is a prime spot, waiting for that big catch. But what if you could increase your chances by knowing exactly where the fish are biting today?

Digital marketing is somewhat like having a sonar system at your disposal. It helps you see where your customers are congregating and understand how best to reach them. This isn't about casting wider nets; it's about casting smarter ones. And in today's digital world, if you're not leveraging these tools, you're likely missing out on a lot of potential catches, i.e., customers.

2.1 Decoding Digital Marketing: What Every Small Business Owner Needs to Know

This section will give you a foundational understanding of digital marketing before we build your specific strategy.

Understanding the Digital Marketing Landscape

The term 'digital marketing' might sound broad and daunting, especially if you're picturing some high-tech operation out of your league. But at its core, digital marketing is about utilizing online channels to promote your business, engage with your customers, and ultimately drive more sales. Just like traditional marketing might use flyers, newspaper ads, or billboards, digital marketing uses tools like websites, social media, emails, and search engines.

Each component of digital marketing is interconnected, forming a web of opportunities that small businesses like yours can tap into. For instance, content you post on social media can drive traffic to your website; email campaigns can be used to follow up on that interest, encouraging reviews or repeat visits; and SEO (Search Engine Optimization) enhances the visibility of all this content on search engines like Google. When used together, these tools create a powerful ecosystem that can significantly amplify your business's online presence and customer reach.

In today's world, having a digital presence is not just beneficial; it's essential. Customers expect to be able to find and interact with businesses online. If they can't find you, or if your online presence doesn't inspire confidence, you risk losing credibility and potentially business. The good news is, digital marketing offers a cost-effective way for you to build that presence, engage with customers, and keep your business competitive in a rapidly evolving marketplace.

Let's get a handle on the terminology and then I'll walk you through a step by step plan to make it easier for customers to find you online, engage with them more effectively, or drive more sales.

The Important Pieces of a Digital Strategy

Now, knowing that these tools exist isn't the same as using them effectively. This is where a solid digital strategy comes into play. A digital strategy acts as your roadmap, guiding you on how to best use digital marketing tools to meet your business goals. Without this strategy, your efforts can be scattered or misaligned with what you're trying to achieve. Think of it as trying to build a house without a blueprint. Sure, you might end up with something resembling a house, but the chances of it being the house you wanted or meeting your needs effectively are slim.

Crafting a digital strategy involves understanding what you want to achieve—be it more brand awareness, more leads, better customer engagement, or all of the above—and then determining which digital tools will best help you meet these goals. It's about being systematic and purposeful with your digital marketing efforts, ensuring that every tweet, every blog post, and every email campaign serves a specific purpose and takes you one step closer to your business objectives.

So, let's cover the tools you'll need to build the right house.

Marketing Channels You'll Want To Become Pretty Darn Familiar With

Facebook:

Facebook, the pioneer of social networking, boasts a staggering user base of over 2.8 billion monthly active users worldwide. Individuals and businesses converge to share a plethora of content formats, including text updates, images, videos, and live streams. With its broad appeal, Facebook attracts users of all ages, but it particularly resonates with the 25-54 demographic. Engaging content on Facebook often includes visually compelling media, such as videos and images, along with interactive elements like polls and user-generated content.

Instagram:

Instagram, a visually immersive platform with over 1 billion monthly active users, is synonymous with aesthetic expression and storytelling. Catering primarily to high-quality images, short videos, stories, and reels, Instagram offers a canvas for creativity and inspiration. Its user base skews towards younger demographics, especially individuals aged 18-34, drawn to its visually curated environment. Authenticity and creativity reign supreme on Instagram, with visually captivating content and genuine narratives driving significant engagement. Strategic use of hashtags and active engagement with followers further enhance the platform's effectiveness for marketers.

X (formerly known as Twitter) :

X, the quintessential microblogging platform, thrives on brevity and real-time conversations. With its 280-character limit, Twitter facilitates rapid-fire exchanges of thoughts, news updates, and trending topics. Its diverse content ecosystem encompasses a wide range of discussions, news updates, memes, and multimedia content. Twitter attracts a diverse user base, with a slight skew towards urban demographics and younger audiences. Timely and relevant content, coupled with the use of hashtags and mentions, drives engagement on Twitter. Visuals, polls, and threaded conversations are also effective tools for fostering interaction.

LinkedIn:

LinkedIn stands as the premier professional networking platform, catering to career development, industry insights, and business networking. With over 774 million members worldwide, LinkedIn serves as a digital hub for professionals across various industries. Content on LinkedIn is geared towards professional updates, thought leadership articles, industry insights, and job postings. The platform appeals predominantly to professionals aged 25-54, particularly those in business, technology, and finance sectors. Educational and informative content, including articles and videos, resonates well on LinkedIn, along with active participation in industry groups and discussions.

YouTube:

YouTube reigns as the undisputed king of online video, boasting over 2 billion logged-in monthly users. As the second-largest search engine after Google, YouTube offers an extensive repository of video content spanning tutorials, vlogs, product reviews, entertainment, and educational content. With its broad demographic appeal, YouTube attracts users of all ages, with a slight skew towards younger demographics. High-quality, engaging video content coupled with attention-grabbing thumbnails and compelling titles drives significant engagement on YouTube. Consistency in content production, interaction with viewers through comments, and collaborations with other creators further enhance engagement levels.

I want to make a special note here that YouTube shorts offer a similar user experience to Instagram and can increase your online visibility without the time commitment of its longer-form content.

TikTok:

With over 1 billion monthly active users, TikTok serves as a creative playground for users to express themselves through entertaining short videos. Its user base skews heavily towards Gen Z and younger Millennials, attracted by its trendsetting culture and bite-sized entertainment. Trendy, authentic, and entertaining content resonates most on TikTok, leveraging popular sounds, hashtags, and participation in challenges to amplify reach and engagement.

Nextdoor:

Nextdoor is primarily utilized by adults aged 30 and above. It serves as a digital space where neighbors can connect, share updates, and exchange recommendations within their immediate vicinity. The platform thrives on content related to neighborhood news, local events, and recommendations for nearby businesses and services. It's an invaluable tool for businesses targeting a hyper-local demographic, allowing them to engage with residents and establish a strong presence within their neighborhood. Optimizing content for

Nextdoor involves creating authentic, community-focused posts that add value to the local audience's daily lives.

Google My Business:

Google My Business (GMB) is a powerful tool for local businesses to establish and manage their online presence across Google's various platforms, including Search and Maps. It allows businesses to showcase essential information such as address, phone number, business hours, and customer reviews. GMB appeals primarily to local businesses seeking to enhance visibility and attract nearby customers. Optimizing GMB profiles with accurate information, high-quality images, and positive customer reviews is key to driving engagement and foot traffic to physical locations.

We could cover dozens more platforms, but most brick-and-mortar businesses can scale and scale fast by just understanding the handful outlined above. This is by no means a course in how to use them, but if you can understand the demographic you'll reach on each platform as well as the type of content that will perform well, you're already leagues ahead of your competitors.

The X's and O's In Your Playbook

If you're a seasoned business owner, you're familiar with the following terms. Still, in addition to understanding the various platforms, you must understand how to use them in the scope of business growth. Getting in front of your ideal clients on those various platforms only works if you have the scaffolding to support that growth behind the scenes. These include tools that allow you to stay engaged with prospects, nurture relationships with people who aren't quite ready to purchase your service, and offer value to the marketplace better than your competition.

Email Marketing:

Email marketing remains a cornerstone of digital communication strategies, allowing businesses to connect directly with their audience through personalized and targeted messages. With email's ubiquitous presence, marketers leverage this channel to nurture leads, drive sales, and build lasting relationships with customers. Email marketing encompasses a variety of content types, including newsletters, promotional offers, transactional emails, and automated drip campaigns. Its versatility makes it suitable for businesses of all sizes and industries, offering a cost-effective way to engage and convert prospects into loyal customers.

CRM (Customer Relationship Manager):

CRM software empowers businesses to centralize customer data, track interactions across various touchpoints, and analyze customer behavior to tailor personalized experiences. By leveraging CRM tools, businesses can streamline sales processes, improve customer service, and foster long-term customer loyalty. A good CRM can save you massive amounts of time nurturing and following up with prospects.

I personally recommend using a product called High Level to host your website and landing pages, manage your customer email and SMS automations, and streamline your operational workflows. This CRM will allow you to easily post on your social media platforms, nurture prospect relationships, and track sales. Here's a link you can click or scan to get a 14-day free trial:

 For full disclosure, I am a HighLevel affiliate, which means I get a commission when purchases are made through this link.

SEO (Search Engine Optimization):

SEO, or Search Engine Optimization, is the practice of optimizing a website to improve its visibility and ranking on search engine results pages (SERPs). By aligning website content, structure, and technical elements with search engine algorithms, businesses aim to increase organic traffic and attract qualified leads. SEO encompasses a range of strategies, including keyword research, on-page optimization, link building, and technical optimization. With the majority of online experiences beginning with a search engine query, SEO is essential for businesses seeking to enhance their online presence and reach their target audience effectively.

Paid Advertising:

Paid advertising encompasses various online advertising channels and formats through which businesses can promote their products or services by paying for ad placement. From search engine advertising, such as Google Ads, to social media advertising, such as Facebook Ads, paid advertising offers a highly targeted and measurable way to reach potential customers. With advanced targeting options and performance tracking capabilities, paid advertising enables businesses to optimize their ad spend and maximize return on investment (ROI).

Organic Content:

Organic content refers to non-paid content created and distributed by businesses to engage their audience and build brand presence organically. This includes blog posts, social media posts, videos, podcasts, and other forms of content designed to resonate with target audiences and provide value. Organic content plays a crucial role in establishing brand authority, nurturing relationships with customers, and driving inbound traffic to owned digital properties. By consistently delivering high-quality, relevant, and engaging content, businesses can attract and retain audiences and solidify their brand persona in the eye of its prospects.

2.2 Laying the Foundation of A Dominating Strategy

Crafting a digital marketing strategy might sound like you need to be a wizard with spreadsheets and analytics, but it's more about understanding your customers and how and when your business will impact them. Remember, marketing at its core is how a business interacts with its marketplace. So take your time to understand these foundational steps of creating a winning strategy better than any competitors, and you're all but guaranteed market domination.

Setting Realistic Goals

The first step in this process is to set clear and realistic goals. This is your opportunity to take control and define what you want your digital marketing efforts to achieve. Are you looking to increase foot traffic to your store, boost online sales, or perhaps improve customer engagement through social media? Defining success for your business is crucial because these goals will guide your actions and help you measure progress. For instance, if your goal is to increase online sales by 20% within the next six months, every part of your digital marketing plan should be geared towards achieving this. This sounds simple, but every single entrepreneur I've worked with gets distracted and, at some point, strays from this principle.

Setting goals for your digital marketing isn't just about saying, "I want more sales." It's about setting goals that are actually useful—goals that guide your efforts and measure your progress. That's where the SMART criteria come into play. SMART stands for Specific, Measurable, Achievable, Relevant, and Time-bound. Each of these factors molds a goal that directs your focus and sharpens your strategies.

Let's break it down using an example from a common goal: increasing sales. A SMART goal here would be to "increase sales by 15% within the next quarter using targeted social media advertising and email promotions." This goal is Specific (it states exactly what you want to achieve), Measurable (it's quantified by a 15% increase), Achievable (it's realistic, assuming you've seen similar growth in past campaigns), Relevant (it supports the broader objective of growing your business), and Time-bound (it has a clear deadline of one quarter). This type of goal not only provides a clear target to aim for but also sets out a timeline that helps keep your marketing efforts on track. It's about making your objectives as clear and actionable as possible, reducing the fog that often surrounds small business's growth efforts.

Knowing Your Market Better Than They Know Themselves

The next step is to understand yourself, your business, and your clients better than anything else. As the CEO or leader of your business, you have to have the clearest vision of where you're going and what you'll personally sacrifice to get there.

Business owners who don't really know their businesses' end goal get distracted by shiny objects and new gizmos and don't understand that when they sway from the course, their employees will lose interest and respect. Just remember you are the only person who will fight for your business at all costs.

More on that later.

As far as understanding your business, you must look at every step of your customer journey with an unbiased, objective eye and ensure your team strives for excellence in every interaction. Cliche, I know.

This is where the hard work comes in. If you take the time to walk through every little detail of your client experience and make an intentional effort to make it a five-star, unbelievable experience, you will have done what one percent of businesses can do.

You will have cracked the marketing code.

Lastly, take a deep dive into your customers - their wants, needs, pain points, and motivations - and don't get caught in the trap of telling them what <u>you</u> want them to hear. You need to understand what <u>they</u> want to hear and give that to them.

I have worked with so many people who have told me they have their client persona dialed in, and then when they write it out on paper, they have targeted about 5 billion of the 7 billion people on this planet. You think that's a good thing—lots of people to purchase your product or service, right? Wrong! If you compete in the masses, you will get lost in the masses.

The market will dictate what gets consumed, and I will tell you right now that if you think you know better than the market, there's no point in reading any further.

Making Smart, Data-Driven Choices

Choosing the right channels is the next critical step. Each digital marketing channel has its strengths and is effective at different stages of the customer journey. You want to select channels not just based on your business goals but also where your target customers are most likely to be found. Think about where your ideal customers spend their time online, what kind of content they consume, and how they prefer to engage with brands. If you're a local bakery, Pinterest and Instagram could be great channels to showcase your creations, while a local plumber might find more success with targeted Google ads and a strong presence on local review sites. Give the market what they want where they want it.

Now, let's talk about budgeting, which can be a pain point if funds are tight. But here's the thing – digital marketing can be tailored to fit almost any budget. The key is to start small and scale up as you see what works. Allocate your initial budget based on what you can afford without putting your business at financial risk, yet don't be afraid to take risks. As mentioned above, set the objective for each platform and know how to measure success. Don't forget that time is also currency. As you start, you'll need to budget both time and money. For example, you might start a blog for SEO benefits, which requires your time, while also experimenting with paid Facebook ads, which require your money. This diversified approach gives you valuable insights into where to invest more down the line.

A good starting point is to consider the main categories of digital marketing expenses:

1. **Ad Spend:** Money directly spent on paid advertising platforms like Google Ads or social media advertising.

2. **Content Creation:** Costs associated with creating content, which might include hiring freelance writers,

graphic designers, or videographers.

3. **Software and Tools:** Monthly or annual fees for using digital marketing tools such as email marketing services, SEO tools, and analytics platforms.

4. **Training and Resources:** Occasionally, you might need to invest in training courses or books to enhance your digital marketing skills.

For each of these categories, get quotes or research average prices to establish a ballpark figure for what you might need to spend. It allows you to allocate funds more accurately and avoid overspending in one area while neglecting another.

Not all marketing channels will yield the same return, and they certainly won't all require the same investment. Prioritization becomes key, especially when funds are limited. Start by assessing each channel's potential return on investment (ROI) in relation to the monetary and time investments. For example, paying $500 for a local NextDoor ad for your plumbing services might bring a better ROI than a free blog post about tankless water heaters. Then again, a free vlog on YouTube on how to DIY paint your kitchen cabinets might bring in more revenue than putting $1000 toward a paid Facebook ad offering a free paint inspection.

Develop a Decision Making/Action Taking Framework

Finally, digital marketing is not a set-it-and-forget-it deal. It requires adjustments and recalibration as your business grows and as market conditions evolve. This isn't a one-off campaign; it's a continuous process that needs to be adjusted and optimized over time. Systematic, regular reviews of your digital marketing goals, budgets, and returns are a necessity when using digital marketing to scale.

Setting a decision making and action taking cadence is essential for keeping your digital marketing efforts on track. Simply put, this means developing a framework for <u>when</u> you look at your data and <u>how</u> you will use it to make decisions.

When starting out, you will want to look at your results every minute of every day. This will drive you insane so it is imperative to be disciplined. Once you're up and running—meaning your ads are running or you're posting consistently—set a cadence for when you'll measure performance. My recommendation is to monitor your results within a 7, 14, and 30-day window. If the results meet KPIs (key performance indicators you set out before launch), don't make changes. If the ROI is not within KPI, adjust as needed and monitor at the same cadence the next month.

This disciplined structure will keep you from getting squirrely and, more importantly, from making rash, emotion-based decisions that can derail your entire strategy. The digital world moves fast, but that doesn't mean chaos prevails. Be prepared to tweak your plan as you learn what works and what doesn't, and keep an eye on how external factors like seasonal trends or competitor actions might affect your progress.

By following these steps—setting clear goals, understanding your market, choosing the right channels, and consistently measuring results that dictate your next move—you'll lay a strong foundation for your digital marketing efforts. This structured approach takes the guesswork out of digital marketing and gives you the control to steer your business toward achieving your online objectives effectively and efficiently.

2.3 Quick Ways to Establish Your Digital Presence

The digital marketplace is bustling, always full of potential customers who are just a few clicks away from discovering your services. But before they can find you, you need to stake out your spot in this digital terrain. Claiming your online space effectively is akin to planting your flag on the moon—it's your way of telling the world, "Here we are, ready to serve."

Claiming Your Online Space

First things first: let's talk about Google My Business. This tool is like the Swiss Army knife of online marketing for local businesses. By setting up and optimizing your Google My Business profile, you're putting your business on the map—literally. When potential customers search for services like yours, you want your business to pop up, complete with your hours, services, and glowing reviews. Make sure you fill out every section of your profile. The more complete your profile, the better Google can match you with potential customers. Also, regularly update your profile with new photos, special offers, and any changes in hours or services. This keeps your business looking active and engaged, which is a green light for customers.

Then, there's social media. Whether it's Facebook, Instagram, or TikTok, these platforms offer a way to connect directly with your audience. But before you start posting, make sure your profiles are fully optimized. This means clear profile pictures, accurate business descriptions, and links to your website. Each platform has its nuances; for instance, Instagram is highly visual, so high-quality photos are a must, whereas LinkedIn often requires a more professional tone and detailed company information.

Lastly, never underestimate the power of a well-designed, functional website. It's often the first serious interaction a potential customer will have with your business. Ensure your website is easy to navigate, mobile-friendly, and fast to load. Every second counts when you're trying to keep a visitor engaged.

You have 3 seconds to make a first impression, so set up your profiles correctly and accurately.

The Power of a Professional Website

Think of your website as your digital storefront. It's where impressions are formed, and decisions are made. Websites that are cluttered, outdated, or slow to load can turn potential customers away faster than a closed sign on your front door. On the other hand, a professional, user-friendly website can work round the clock to attract and retain customers.

Key elements of a successful small business website include a clear description of who you are and what you do, an easy-to-navigate layout, and a strong call to action—whether that's making a purchase, booking a service, or contacting you for more details. Also, include customer testimonials and case studies to build trust and credibility. These elements reassure potential customers that choosing your business is the right choice.

SEO is another critical component of your website strategy. By optimizing your site with relevant keywords, you ensure that your business shows up in search results when potential customers are looking for the services you offer. Moreover, adding a blog can significantly boost your SEO efforts. Regular posts about topics relevant to your business not only keep your website content fresh but also help establish you as an authority in your field.

Social Media Quick Starts

For many small businesses, social media is a blessing and a curse. However, it doesn't have to be. Start with one platform where your customers are most likely to be. For example, if you're in a visually oriented business like landscaping or cake decorating, Instagram might be your best start. Post high-quality pictures of your work, share customer testimonials, and offer quick tips or insights into your process.

Engagement is key. Respond to comments, messages, and reviews as promptly as possible. This interaction not only builds relationships but also signals to the platform algorithms that your page is active, boosting your visibility. Additionally, utilize the tools each platform offers, such as hashtags on Instagram or Facebook groups related to your industry, to increase your reach and connect with more potential customers.

Online Directories and Reviews

Local directories are often overlooked in the digital marketing game, yet they can be goldmines of credibility and visibility. Platforms like Yelp, TripAdvisor, and even local business groups or chambers of commerce can help put your business on the radar of local customers. Make sure your business information is consistent across all directories—discrepancies can confuse potential customers and hurt your SEO.

Reviews are the lifeblood of local businesses. Positive reviews not only enhance your reputation but also improve your visibility. Encourage satisfied customers to leave a review by making the process as simple as possible—provide links via QR codes in your office or via links in your emails to your Google My Business profile or other review sites. If you are not already prioritizing getting reviews, make this priority number one.

Address negative reviews promptly and professionally, showing that you value customer feedback and are committed to improving service. Be authentic because your response to a bad review weighs ten times as much as your response to a positive one to a potential customer. Remember, each review, good or bad, is an opportunity to showcase your customer service level.

By taking these steps to establish and enhance your digital presence, you're not just setting up shop in the digital marketplace; you're opening the door to endless opportunities for growth and connection. Whether through a robust Google My Business profile, an engaging social media presence, a professional website, or leveraging local directories and reviews, each element plays a crucial role in how your business is perceived online and, ultimately, in your bottom line.

As we wrap up this chapter, remember that your digital presence is your global handshake. It's how you introduce your business to potential customers and start building relationships. Each step you take to enhance this presence brings you closer to achieving visibility, credibility, and trust in a digital-first world. We will dive into more specific strategies to optimize these channels and truly make your digital presence work for you in later chapters, but first, let's continue laying foundation.

3

Knowing Who The F**k You Are

Yeah, the title of this chapter may seem a little *intense*. It's supposed to be. Understanding your identity as a business owner, your core values, your vision, and the impression you want to leave on your community is crucial. These form the bedrock of your business, yet they're often neglected, and few people understand how they relate to great marketing strategies.

In big Corporate America, there's an understanding that you will go in, do some work, and leave for the day, never really knowing if what you spent eight hours doing actually makes a difference at the company. But what you spend your eight hours doing in mom-and-pop small businesses matters! You can legitimately see your progress from week to week and month to month and know you are making a difference.

The long and short of it is that if you choose to become a business owner, you are choosing to be a leader, you are choosing to become a better version of yourself, and you are choosing to forge a path where there was none. You, my friend, have chosen the craziest path of them all.

If you haven't yet done significant work to understand who you are and who you want to be, let this be your sign to take the time to go through each section of this chapter. Without this foundation, you cannot expect anyone to believe in your vision, let alone respect and follow you in pursuit of it.

Going through this exercise will be one of the greatest things you ever do for yourself and your business.

3.1 What Do You Stand For?

What are the values that you hold most dear?

This is the part where you say something like "integrity," "resilience," and "honesty." These are great, but I challenge you to think deeper than just what you hope someone puts in your eulogy. Think about how you'd characterize your desire to serve others in your community, your desire to grow your business or describe your approach to challenges. Everyone writes "integrity" in their company motto, but too often, that value doesn't ring true. What you determine as a core value can't be lip service. These values have to be the things you will never budge on, the things that, when business gets tough, will anchor you, and the things you will fire people over.

Take a few minutes to determine your top three to five values or pillars on which you live and run your business.

Once you have spent time thinking of your core values, it's time to give them some context. Those values you chose are great, but you have to put context behind them because I can tell you 1000% that your definition of honesty and that of the sixteen-year-old kid you hire as your third employee will be vastly different.

Think of a defining moment that led you to adopt those values. Then, turn that story into a short characterization of how that value should play out in your business.

Once your values have context, your employees can relate them to their lives and workplace experiences and buy into the mission. This context also shows customers and prospects what they can expect when working with you, and believe it or not, this clarity and genuineness will bring you business and make it stay.

Don't search the internet for the best value statements or companies with the coolest culture. You have to pull these values from your own life. They have to mean something to you and be something you will hold firm on when things get tough.

3.2 What Is the Dream?

Now, it's time to articulate your dream and the reason you started your business. Then, we'll determine what it will take to get there.

Start this section by taking a few moments to answer the following:

- Why did you start your business in the first place?
- What is your goal with the business - both your monetary and personal goals?
- What makes you get up in the morning and keep going back?
- When you envision the finish line, what does your business look like?
- When you envision the finish line, who is there with you?
- What's been the biggest challenge keeping you from getting to that vision?
- What new skills do you need to acquire to accomplish

your dream?

- How bad do you want it? Would it be nice if you made it there, or would you feel like an absolute failure if you didn't make it to that endpoint?

- Are you doing what you must do today, this week, and this month to achieve your goal?

When you answer these, answer with the most blunt, factual response you can. Don't sugarcoat this. Don't embellish. If you aren't extremely honest with yourself about these answers, everything you build from here on out will be built on quicksand.

Additionally, it will be a massive disservice to yourself if you respond with phrases like, "I want to make a million dollars a year" and, "I only want to work two days a week." Your end goal must have a worthwhile and personal impact on your life so that you can pursue it at all costs.

The other critical piece is that you have to be humble. My biggest pet peeve is when I would get answers like, "I want to have three locations doing $1M per year each." But when asked what skills they'd need to acquire, they'd say, "I've owned this business for twenty years, I'm the biggest player in my area, I know what I'm doing." That was always the beginning of the end because these people didn't realize that if there's no motivation or desire to get better, you'll stay stagnant at best.

This dream has to become so real in your mind that you feel it is your inevitable reality. It has to have specific attributes that tell your mind it's real. This dream has to be something that you will pursue at all costs and not just hope you'll accomplish it.

You have to give it life.

3.3 What Environment Will You Create?

Once you have clarity on what you stand for and what you're aiming at, you must ensure you create an environment and surround yourself with people who will help you achieve your goals.

This is often the most challenging part because once people are in front of us, we build relationships with them that often lead us to overemphasize their needs above our own. To value others' aspirations in balance with your own is the ultimate measure of good leadership.

You must understand that your employees are humans in good faith doing their best to live a good life and provide for themselves and their families. However, you are doing the same. Except you've taken on the financial and personal responsibility to grow a business that you know can have an amazing impact on those you love and those in your community.

Whether bringing on a partner or hiring a teenager for part-time work over the summer, there cannot be a shade of doubt or an ounce of uncertainty about what kind of culture they are saying yes to when they accept the role. There cannot be any uncertainty about what they are responsible for, and they have to embody the core values you laid out.

It's fine if a candidate wants to clock in and get a paycheck; it's just not okay in your business.

Your primary role as a leader is to obsess over your culture and hold the highest standard when it comes to the people you hire. You are responsible for maintaining your culture at all times and recognizing when something or someone may affect it.

3.4 Limiting Beliefs

If you aren't familiar with what a limiting belief is, the concept is fairly straightforward. It is a belief you have about yourself or your situation of why something cannot or will not happen.

For example, you might say, "I'm not disciplined enough to have a bodybuilder's physique." In reality, you have the ability to have a very disciplined exercise routine and diet, hire a coach, oil yourself down, fake tan until you're an unsightly orange color, and dawn a thong bikini; you just tell yourself you cannot do it.

The most unfortunate part about limiting beliefs is that we make them so real in our minds that our bodies and behaviors react as if they are, in fact, real.

That belief that you're unable to achieve the Herculean physique leads you to make choices and take actions that align with that belief. It starts with your internal thoughts about who you are and what you're capable of. You tell yourself you cannot learn how to eat right or lift weights. Then, your actions align with those thoughts. Instead of eating chicken and broccoli at home, you swing by the local burger joint a few times a week. This behavior then provides feedback to your brain and body that you are just this way, and thus, your limiting belief is strengthened.

It's a downward spiral that keeps you stuck. If you're going to make marketing, or anything new, work for you, you will have to constantly confront your limiting beliefs and consciously form new neural pathways that teach your mind the opposite.

You may feel this has become a self-help book, but I'm going off the beaten path here for a legitimate reason. The most successful entrepreneurs I've worked with approach learning new marketing skills as if they were five-year-olds on their first field trip to the museum. They lose all constraints, have to play with everything, break a few things, and by the end of the trip, they're in a competition with their best friend about who learned more.

These kids don't have limiting beliefs like, "I've got nothing to learn from the museum" or, "I'm too old to learn anything new." Instead, they say, "Hey, that's new; I need to go figure that out."

Somewhere along the way, we lose that innate sense of exploration and learning due to our fear of failing and the constant cycle of telling ourselves we will fail.

So, how do you fix these limiting beliefs?

You've defined your dream a few sections above this point. Now, it's time to start living according to what it takes to achieve that dream. That, and start being a kid again. View life through the lens of learning, and don't be afraid of failure.

It's easier said than done, but you're going to act according to your dreams or your fears—your choice.

3.5 What Are You Willing To Give Up To Get Where You Want To Go?

Before we dive into this section and you find yourself on the therapist's couch, let me lay some groundwork for you.

This is the differentiator between good businesses and great businesses.

This is the section where you must take a cold, hard look in the mirror and recognize that YOU have some work to do.

If you can't accept that you are the weakest link in your business, you are the one with the most work to be done, and you have to become a better version of yourself, stop reading this book. Stop wasting your time.

Typically, when I ask a business owner, "What are you willing to give up to get where you want to go?" they say something like, "I need to give up procrastinating," or, "I need to give up the coaching group I'm in since it's not helping me," or, "I need to give up hiring my family members."

Eh. Wrong.

What they, and perhaps you, really need to give up is:

1. Thinking that everyone else has something to learn, but you don't.

2. Holding a mediocre standard in your personal and professional lives.

3. Allowing any, and I mean any, excuse to come in the way of you and your dreams.

4. Surrounding yourself with people who don't push you

to be better.

5. Having a loser's mindset.

6. False beliefs that this will work for someone else but not you.

Essentially, what you need to be willing to give up in pursuit of your dreams is an old version of yourself that doesn't suit you anymore. Remember that whole section about making your dream so real that it becomes your reality? It's the same concept for yourself. The difference is you have to start changing your core being, and this is the hardest f**king part.

How do you start to become someone else?

You get extremely clear on your weaknesses and work day and night to make them strengths.

For example, if you have a fear of spending money in the early stages of your business and you doubt yourself in making big strategic decisions, your answer needs to be something like this:

"I need to give up the fear of spending money on my business. I will research how much money Warren Buffet, Jeff Bezos, and Gary V spent on their businesses in the first two years. I will identify the three most significant things I need to spend money on and determine precisely what I will do and the timeframe I will do it in to get those three things to return on my investment."

Then you do it.

In my experience, the most common thing people need to give up is the comfort of making a decent living in order to make a great life. Many small business owners start to get stale and apathetic when they start making a comfortable living. Don't get me wrong, they are still working hard and are hanging their hat up each day on something they can be proud of. But that's precisely the problem. They've decided in their mind that they're okay with that amount of "hard work" and that the return is "good enough."

But what if you didn't settle for good enough, defined what a great life meant, and didn't stop until you got that?

A great life could mean making a good income, but you do it passively while your employees run your daily operations. It may mean you make all of Johnny's soccer games and Susie's dance recitals, and you don't budge, negotiate, or default on that promise in any way. Ever. If that were your definition of a great life, you wouldn't hesitate to spend the money on another employee, blink about spending 100 days straight of going to bed at 2 am to perfect your operations or make your team spend two hours a day practicing their sales pitch.

Knowing who you are and what you stand for and believing so deeply in achieving your dream is the difference between running a good business and creating a legacy.

4

Building Your Brand Online

In the bustling digital marketplace, <u>your brand is your promise to your customer</u>.

It tells them what they can expect from your products and services and differentiates your offerings from those of your competitors. Your brand is derived from who you are, who you want to be, and who people perceive you to be. You've just done a lot of work to help you solidify the 'who you are' and 'who you want to be' parts, but this section is about knowing your market.

Are you truly aware of who is actually interacting with your brand online? Understanding your online audience can dramatically shift your digital marketing strategy from shooting in the dark to making precise, informed decisions that drive engagement and sales. This is crucial for you, the small business owner, who must optimize every minute and every dollar spent to ensure maximum return on investment.

4.1 The Importance of Knowing Your Online Audience

Identifying Your Audience

The first step in mastering your online marketing is to clearly define who your audience is. You're not just looking to attract anyone to your business; you're looking for people who are most likely to become customers and, eventually, loyal advocates of your brand. To do this effectively, start by gathering data on your current customers. Look at who is buying from you, who is following you on social media, and who is subscribing to your newsletters.

Tools like Google Analytics can provide invaluable insights into your website traffic and help you understand key demographics such as age, gender, and location. Also, pay attention to customer feedback and reviews—they can tell you a lot about who your customers are and what they need and expect from your business.

Creating Buyer Personas

Once you've identified who your customers are, the next step is to create detailed buyer personas. These are fictional, yet detailed representations of your ideal customers. They help you understand your customers (and potential customers) better, making it easier for you to tailor your content, messaging, and services to meet their specific needs, behaviors, and concerns.

When defining your client you need to put yourself in their shoes. You need to know them as if they were a family member. What are their fears, motivations and barriers? What are their interests and how do they spend their hard earned money? What are their pain points? What are their turn offs?

Ideally, each persona should include demographic details, behavior patterns, motivations, and goals. The more detailed you are, the better.

For instance, instead of a generic customer profile, you might have 'DIY Dan,' a 36-year-old homeowner who likes to tackle home improvement projects on his own and often looks for how-to videos and quality tools. He's got some discretionary funds to use on home renovations, but he's also conscious of not breaking the bank. He has basic home improvement knowledge but does these kinds of projects as a hobby and knows where his limit is. If a project takes more than a weekend, he knows it will go unfinished for months, and his wife will nag him endlessly to complete it. Understanding Dan's motivations and challenges can help you create marketing messages that speak directly to him, perhaps by highlighting your expert advice on completing projects efficiently and working within a range of budgets.

Engaging with Your Audience

Knowing where your prospective buyers spend their time online, and the type of content they consume can significantly enhance your engagement rates. Engage with your audience by creating content that they find valuable, which can range from educational articles and how-to videos to interactive polls or behind-the-scenes glimpses of your business. Remember, engagement is a two-way street; it's about dialogue, not monologue. Respond to comments, participate in discussions, and actively ask your audience for their opinions or needs. This not only increases engagement but also builds trust and loyalty.

Using Analytics Tools

To effectively measure how well your engagement strategies are working, you'll need to use analytics tools. These tools can help you track which types of content perform best, which platforms are most effective for your brand, and where you should focus your marketing efforts moving forward. For example, Facebook Insights can provide detailed metrics about your social media posts' reach and engagement, while Google Analytics can show you how visitors find your site and what they do once they're there. By regularly reviewing this data, you can continuously refine and optimize your digital marketing strategies, ensuring that they deliver the best possible results.

By deeply understanding who your online audience is, what they care about, and how they interact with digital content, you can create more targeted, effective marketing strategies. These strategies not only increase your visibility and attractiveness as a brand but also drive deeper engagement, turning casual browsers into loyal customers. In the next sections, we'll delve deeper into how you can leverage this understanding to craft a compelling online presence that resonates with your target audience, differentiates your brand in the marketplace, and ultimately, drives business growth.

4.2 Establishing Your Brand Voice & Visual Presence Online

Crafting a compelling brand presence requires balancing visual aesthetics with engaging messaging. Your brand's visual identity speaks volumes, capturing attention and conveying the essence of your business within seconds. From the colors of your logo to the imagery on your website, every visual element shapes the perception of your brand in the minds of your audience.

But visuals are only part of the equation. Establishing your brand voice is equally critical. It's about defining the personality and tone of your business—how you speak to your audience and the emotions you evoke. Whether aiming for approachable friendliness or authoritative professionalism, your brand voice should resonate with your target demographic. By harmonizing your visual branding and brand voice, you lay the foundation for a compelling online presence that captivates audiences and fosters lasting connections with your brand.

How To Find Your Brand Voice

When you think about your business interacting with customers, it's not just what you say but how you say it that leaves a lasting impression. Your brand voice is the personality and emotion infused into your company's communications. It should be consistent across all content because it reflects your company's values and connects with your audience on a personal level. Identifying and refining your brand voice isn't just a task—it's an ongoing process that can significantly influence how your audience perceives your brand.

First step, identifying your brand voice involves a deep dive into what your business stands for—its values, its mission, and the feelings you want to evoke in your customers. Are you aiming to appear friendly and approachable, or professional and authoritative? Perhaps you value humor and wit, or maybe sincerity and reliability are your cornerstones. You know all that work you did in the previous chapter? That all comes into play here. Your brand voice doesn't typically stray too far from your personal perspective or characteristics, but it may have some unique or individual features. Maybe your brand is funnier than you, less blunt than you, or is more outgoing. Define who you are <u>and</u> separately define who your brand is.

Think about how your favorite brands communicate. What makes their voice distinctive? Use these reflections as a baseline to craft a voice that resonates with your audience and enhances your brand's personality.

Once you've sketched a clear picture of your desired brand voice, it's time to put it into practice. Consistency here is crucial. Imagine you're crafting a social media post, a blog entry, or an email newsletter. Each piece should sound like it came from the same source. Inconsistent messaging can confuse your audience and dilute your brand identity. To avoid this, create a style guide that outlines your brand's tone, the dos and don'ts, and even common phrases or words typical of your brand. This guide will be invaluable, especially as your team grows or when outsourcing content creation.

Here are some examples of recognizable and distinct brand voices:

Disney

Disney's brand voice is magical, family-friendly, and whimsical, focusing on storytelling and creating enchanting experiences. Their messaging emphasizes imagination and the joy of bringing beloved characters to life.

Old Spice

Old Spice is known for its humorous, confident, and quirky voice, using over-the-top humor and unconventional commercials. Their memorable ads often feature eccentric spokespersons and bizarre, yet funny, scenarios.

Apple

Apple's brand voice is innovative, sleek, and minimalist, consistently highlighting simplicity, elegance, and cutting-edge technology. Their communication is clear and focused, with a strong emphasis on design and user experience.

Another critical aspect is adapting your brand voice to different platforms while maintaining its core identity. Each social media platform has its own unique environment and audience expectations. For instance, LinkedIn is a professional network where a more formal tone might be necessary, whereas Instagram is often more casual and visual. The trick is to slightly tweak your voice to fit the platform's context without losing the essence of what makes your brand voice unique. This might mean presenting the same message in a slightly different way. For example, a professional consultation service might post a detailed, informative article on LinkedIn about industry trends and share a quick, engaging tip related to those trends on Twitter.

Engagement through your brand voice is about making real connections. It's not enough to broadcast messages to your audience; you should also encourage interaction and foster a sense of community. Use your brand voice to ask questions, respond to comments, and participate in discussions. Show empathy where needed and appreciation often. This active engagement helps to humanize your brand and build loyalty and trust among your audience. Remember, the most loyal customers are often those who feel directly connected and valued by the brands they support.

By establishing a strong, consistent, and adaptable brand voice, you not only enhance your brand's identity but also create deeper connections with your audience. These connections can turn casual browsers into loyal customers and loyal customers into advocates for your brand. As you continue to refine your voice and adapt to new platforms and trends, always keep your core values and audience at the heart of your communications. This focus will ensure your brand voice remains a powerful asset in your digital marketing arsenal, helping you stand out in a crowded marketplace and build lasting relationships with your customers.

How Does Your Brand Handle Negativity

No matter how stellar your services are or how diligently you work, facing negative reviews is an inevitable part of doing business in the digital age. It's not just about the occasional dissatisfied customer; it's about how these incidents can impact your online reputation and, ultimately, your bottom line. However, negative reviews also present a unique opportunity to showcase your commitment to customer service and to turn potential pitfalls into powerful demonstrations of your business's values.

Negative reviews are inevitable, but how you handle them makes all the difference.

Addressing feedback, particularly complaints, swiftly and efficiently shows your customers they are valued. The digital age has accelerated expectations for rapid responses, and a delayed reply can sometimes be as damaging as a negative review. Establish protocols for timely responses, ensuring no customer query goes unanswered for long. This promptness in addressing issues helps manage potential fallout and demonstrates your commitment to customer satisfaction. When handled correctly, even the most critical feedback can be turned into a showcase of your company's dedication to its customers.

Turning complaints into opportunities for growth is an art every small business owner should master. Each complaint provides a unique insight into areas of your business that may need improvement. For instance, if a customer complains about a delayed service, it might highlight a need for better time management or customer communication protocols. Address these issues head-on by first acknowledging the customer's inconvenience and then outlining the steps you're taking to prevent future occurrences. This not only rectifies the immediate issue but also enhances your operational strategies, potentially preventing future complaints of a similar nature. Moreover, publicly handling complaints gracefully can turn a potentially negative situation into a testament to your business's integrity and commitment to customer satisfaction.

Public and private channels each offer distinct advantages for handling complaints. Social media and public forums allow you to address issues in a way that is visible to other customers, showcasing your proactive approach. Be genuine and empathetic in your responses if that is true to your brand voice, and remember that how you handle negative reviews speaks volumes about your business.

How To Create An Impactful Visual Presence

In the realm of digital marketing, the power of visual consistency cannot be overstated. When your business presents itself online, every visual element, from your logo to your social media graphics, plays a crucial role in building your brand identity. Consider this: when a potential customer encounters your brand online, you have only a few seconds to make an impression. In these brief moments, your colors, fonts, and imagery can communicate more about your business than words ever could. A consistent visual style across all your digital platforms reinforces your brand's identity and fosters a sense of familiarity and trust among your audience. This consistency tells your customers that you are reliable and professional, qualities that are particularly important for small businesses competing in a crowded market.

Visual consistency helps create a seamless experience for users interacting with your brand across various online platforms. Whether they are scrolling through your Instagram, reading a tweet, or browsing your website, the uniform use of visual elements makes your brand instantly recognizable.

This recognition is vital in a digital landscape where attention is fleeting, and first impressions are lasting. For example, suppose your business uses a specific shade of blue in your logo. In that case, that same shade should appear in other visual elements such as your website header, social media profiles, and email newsletters. Consistency in visuals enhances brand recall, which is crucial when it comes time for a customer to make a purchasing decision.

Logos of some of the most well-known global brands

Do you recognize the brands associated with these four logos? Of course, you do!

Although none of these are official logos, you could instantly name which business they were associated with. When looking at the faux Starbucks or Apple logos, you might also conjure up images of people with their laptops sunk into cozy chairs of earthy colors or the unboxing of the latest modern, sleek, and metallic iPhone. This is the power of visual consistency; the brand has a distinct feel and voice.

Now, if you looked at the images and had a smell come back to you — roasting coffee or salty french fries — or perhaps a feeling — opening your first iPhone or wearing your new Jordans — you just experienced the exponential power of visual consistency. When simple images can evoke moderately good to amazingly positive emotions in consumers, you have brand attachment and, ultimately, loyalty.

Choosing Your Visual Elements

Selecting the right colors, fonts, and imagery for your brand is not just about personal preference; it's about what best communicates the personality and values of your business to your target audience. Colors evoke emotions and associations — blue can convey trust and dependability, red can signal energy and passion, and green often represents growth and health. Choose a color palette that reflects the feelings you want to associate with your business. Similarly, the fonts you choose can say a lot about your brand. A traditional serif font might communicate that you are established and respectable, while a sleek sans-serif font could convey a modern and approachable feel.

Imagery also plays a critical role in defining your brand. The images you select should represent your target audience and the ethos of your brand. If you're a local gym, images of real people from your gym could be more effective than stock photos of generic fitness scenes. These authentic visuals personalize your brand and help form a connection with potential customers who can see themselves in those pictures. High-quality images are crucial; they reflect the quality of your business. Remember, in the digital world, your visuals might be the first and only chance to impress potential customers.

Brand Guidelines

To maintain visual consistency, it's wise to develop a set of brand guidelines. These guidelines should detail your color palette, font styles, logo usage, and the overall tone of your imagery. They serve as a reference for anyone who creates digital content for your business, ensuring that everything from your website to your social media posts aligns with your brand identity. Brand guidelines help maintain consistency, which is crucial not only for brand recognition but also for brand reliability in the eyes of your customers.

Creating detailed brand guidelines might seem daunting, especially for small businesses with limited resources, but it doesn't have to be overly complicated. Start with the basics—define your colors, fonts, and logo usage. Use a free tool like Canva to get inspiration and quickly develop your brand guide. As your business grows and your marketing efforts expand, you can develop more detailed guidelines covering a wider content range.

The investment of time and effort into creating these guidelines will pay dividends by making your brand stronger and more cohesive across all digital platforms.

Leveraging Multimedia

In today's digital marketing, static images alone might not be enough to capture the attention of your audience. This is where multimedia comes into play. Videos, animations, and interactive graphics can significantly enhance your brand's visual appeal and engagement. Videos are particularly powerful tools for storytelling. They can convey your brand's message in a dynamic, engaging way that static images and text cannot. A well-produced video that tells a compelling story about your business can leave a lasting impression on viewers.

Moreover, incorporating multimedia content into your digital marketing strategy can also improve your SEO (Search Engine Optimization) efforts. Search engines favor content-rich websites, and by including videos and interactive graphics, you can boost your site's search rankings, making it easier for potential customers to find you.

The reality is that video is king. If you are not willing to be on video or are uncomfortable asking your employees to be on video, you are making it exponentially harder for your business to reach your market impactfully. Get comfortable talking about your service, business, and personal story in the mirror, and making video content will become second nature.

Incorporating multimedia does not necessarily require a big budget. Many small business owners worry about the perceived high costs of video production, but with today's technology, creating high-quality video content has never been more accessible. A smartphone with a good camera, a basic video editing app, and a content creation plan are all that's needed to create engaging video content that resonates with your audience.

Here are some of my recommended pieces of equipment that you either already have or can easily buy online:

1. iPhone 7 or higher

2. 10" ring light WITH the phone holder

3. Bluetooth clip-on microphone

In summary, the visual elements of your brand are not just decorative. They are fundamental components of your digital marketing strategy, playing a crucial role in how customers perceive and interact with your brand online. By carefully selecting these elements, maintaining consistency through brand guidelines, and effectively leveraging multimedia, you can create a strong, recognizable brand that stands out in the digital marketplace. This not only attracts more customers but also builds a level of trust and loyalty that is essential for the success of any small business in today's competitive landscape.

4.3 Crafting Your Unique Selling Proposition Online

Defining your Unique Selling Proposition (USP) is not just about standing out in a crowded market. It's about creating a compelling reason for customers to choose you and stay loyal to your brand. In the digital arena, where competition is just a click away, a well-defined USP is not just beneficial; it's a game-changer that can elevate your business to new heights.

Think about what makes your business stand out. Is it your decade-long experience, the personalized touch you add to each project, or perhaps your commitment to using only the highest-quality materials? Maybe it's your speedy service, your innovative solutions, or your community involvement. Whatever it is, it needs to resonate not just as different but as decidedly better or uniquely appealing to your audience. Remember, a good USP clearly answers the question, "Why should I choose you?"

Once you've identified your USP, the challenge lies in communicating it effectively. Your website is a great starting point. It's often the first place potential customers go to check you out, and if what makes you unique isn't immediately clear, you might lose them to the next tab over—your competitor. Your homepage should prominently feature your USP, ideally above the fold where visitors can see it without scrolling. Use engaging, concise language and, where appropriate, support it with visuals. For example, if your USP is the durability of your products, a video or graphic comparing the lifespan of your product to average competitors can be very effective.

Social media is another crucial platform for broadcasting your USP. Each platform offers different tools for emphasizing what sets you apart. On Instagram, for example, you can use stories to showcase real-time behind-the-scenes looks at your processes or highlight customer testimonials. On LinkedIn, articles or posts that delve into your expertise and track record can help establish your authority in the field. Remember, consistency is key across all platforms. Your USP should be clear and consistent whether a customer is browsing your Instagram, reading a tweet, or perusing your LinkedIn profile.

Integrating your USP into all aspects of your digital marketing isn't just about repetition, though. It's about making sure it's woven into every part of your customer's digital interaction with your business. From the email newsletters you send out to the blog posts on your website, from PPC ads to the descriptions of your YouTube videos. Each piece of content should reinforce what makes you the best choice.

Understanding and deploying your USP effectively can transform your online presence. It turns your digital platforms into more than just places to contact you or learn about your services; it turns them into compelling, persuasive tools that communicate the unique value of your business. This not only attracts more customers but helps ensure they choose you over the competition, time and again. As you move forward, keep refining and revisiting your USP. Markets evolve, and so should your approach to ensuring you remain as relevant and attractive to potential customers as the day you started.

Offers v. Promotions

Lastly, let's talk about leveraging your USP with special promotions.

Before diving too deep, I want to make a distinction between your offer and your promotions.

Understanding the distinction between your offer and your promotions is crucial for effectively engaging potential customers and driving sales. An offer represents the value proposition a business extends to its clients when purchasing its products or services. It encapsulates the unique benefits and advantages that differentiate the business from its competitors. On the other hand, promotions are the strategic approach employed by the business to capture the attention of prospects and entice them to explore further.

Promotions are powerful tools for converting interest into sales. However, the trick is not just creating an intriguing promotion but one that perfectly aligns with your USP. For instance, if your USP is a personalized service, a promo providing a free consultation session before any commitment is made can be more appealing than a simple percentage discount. It reaffirms your commitment to personal service, aligning the promotion with your overall brand promise.

The key to crafting successful promotions lies in being concise, eye-catching, and compelling enough to halt a viewer's scrolling. It's about grabbing attention and piquing curiosity in a succinct yet impactful manner. Let's break it down further using an example from the HVAC industry.

Imagine a heating and cooling company that prides itself on offering peace of mind, delivering exponential savings, and providing expertise from local professionals when replacing HVAC units. These elements constitute the core offer – the promise made to customers who opt for their services.

Now, the promotion serves as the vehicle to draw potential customers in and make them aware of this enticing offer. It needs to be attention-grabbing and aligned with the overarching brand message. For instance, the promotion could be a free HVAC system assessment or a substantial discount of $900 off a new HVAC unit.

In this scenario, the offer of peace of mind and local expertise is reinforced by the promotion of a complimentary assessment, showcasing the company's commitment to ensuring customer satisfaction and peace of mind throughout the HVAC replacement process. Alternatively, the substantial discount serves as a tangible incentive for customers to take action, capitalizing on the promise of exponential savings while highlighting the company's affordability and value proposition.

Building Your Promotions

Promotions act as the dynamic force propelling engagement and conversion. Let's explore how to strategically build promotions that complement your core service offering, captivate your target audience, and ultimately drive growth and loyalty for your business in today's competitive market landscape.

Below are the most common promotional hooks in advertising, accompanied by some examples:

Introductory Promotions

Includes special discounts or packages for first-time customers to incentivize them to try the service.

- HVAC Company: 20% off your first HVAC maintenance service for new customers.

- Med Spa: First-time customers receive a complimentary facial with any skincare treatment.

Free Consultations or Low-Cost Assessments

Offers complimentary or low-cost consultations to help prospects understand the value and benefits of the service.

- Massage Business: Free 30-minute massage consultation to assess individual needs and preferences.

- Dentist: $49 oral health assessment, including X-rays for new patients.

Money-Back Guarantees

Assures customers of satisfaction by offering a money-back guarantee if they are not satisfied with the service.

- Chiropractor: Guaranteed to help you reduce or eliminate the use of pain medications or your money back.

- Roofer: Money-back guarantee if the roofing repair work does not meet NRCA quality standards.

Bundle Deals

Combines multiple services at a discounted rate to encourage customers to purchase more services.

- Dental Clinic: Comprehensive dental cleaning and whitening package at a discounted rate.

- Roofing Company: Roof repair and gutter cleaning bundle with 15% off both services.

Seasonal Promotions:

Offers special promotions or discounts during holidays or seasons when demand for certain services may be higher.

- HVAC Company: Summer AC tune-up special - 25% off regular maintenance during the summer season.

- Med Spa: Winter skincare package including hydrating treatments at a discounted rate.

Limited-Time or Limited-Number Offers

Creates a sense of urgency by promoting time-limited offers or promotions that are limited in quantity.

- Massage Business: Flash sale - Book any massage within the next 48 hours and get 20% off.

- Dentist: Teeth whitening special - The next ten people to call our office and schedule their appointment lock in 30% off.

Low-Cost or No-Cost Starts

Offers a low-cost entry point for potential customers to try out the service or product, allowing them to experience its value without a significant financial commitment upfront.

- Landscaper: Free first mow when you sign up for monthly services.

- Med Spa: Enroll in our signature weight loss program for just $1 down.

The keys to successful promotions are ensuring your market wants the offer and putting it on the platforms your prospects use.

Ultimately, the synergy between offers and promotions is paramount in driving conversions and cultivating customer loyalty. By aligning promotions with the core offer and effectively communicating the unique benefits to prospective customers, small businesses can leverage these marketing tactics to their advantage, fostering meaningful connections and driving growth in the digital landscape.

As we close this chapter on building your brand online, remember that your digital presence is more than just a marketing tool. It's a reflection of your business ethos, your commitment to your customers, and your adaptability in the face of feedback. The strategies discussed here—from understanding your audience to managing online negativity—form the pillars upon which a resilient and respected online brand is built. In the next chapter, we'll explore how to leverage digital strategies to not just sustain but actively grow your business in the competitive online marketplace.

5

Winning Strategies for Social Media

In this chapter, I'll dive into the practical aspects of social media strategy for small businesses. Instead of overwhelming you with the complexities of every platform, I'll focus on simplifying content planning, streamlining audience engagement, and distinguishing between paid and organic strategies. My goal is to equip you with the tools to make strategic choices that maximize your marketing efforts without spreading yourself too thin across the digital landscape.

5.1 Make Content Planning Simple

When running a small brick and mortar business, time is a commodity you can't afford to waste, especially on social media. Yet, maintaining a robust online presence is crucial to staying competitive and relevant in today's market. The good news? There are strategies and tools designed to streamline your social media management so it supports your business without overwhelming your schedule. Let's dive into how to efficiently plan and manage your social media content.

Competitor Analysis

Never underestimate the importance of keeping an eye on your competitors. Observing how your competitors use social media can provide valuable insights into what might or might not work for your business. If you see a competitor finding great engagement through interactive polls on Twitter or live videos on Facebook, consider how you might incorporate similar strategies in a way that aligns with your brand voice and goals.

Competitor analysis isn't about imitation but rather about learning from the landscape. It's about seeing what's out there and then carving out your unique spot in the digital marketplace. This kind of strategic observation can help you make informed decisions about where to invest your social media efforts and how to differentiate your brand effectively.

Content Calendars

Creating a content calendar is like mapping out a blueprint for your social media activity. It helps you organize when and what you will post, ensuring that your content is varied, consistent, and timed perfectly to engage your audience.

Start by marking important dates that are relevant to your business—this could be seasonal events, promotions, or local community events. From there, plan out your posts to coincide with these dates, filling in the gaps with regular content that engages and informs your customers. This not only keeps your content relevant and timely but also gives you a clear view of your marketing efforts over the year, making it easier to manage without last-minute scrambles for post ideas. Check out the free, follow-along guide for an easy to follow content calendar.

Batch Creation and Scheduling

One of the most time-efficient strategies in social media management is creating and scheduling your content in batches. Dedicate a day or two each month to create all your content for the next few weeks. This might include writing posts, creating graphics, or filming short videos. Once your content is ready, use scheduling tools like Buffer or Hootsuite to schedule posts across different social media platforms. This approach not only saves you time but also ensures that your social media feeds remain active and engaging, even on your busiest days.

Batching also allows you to maintain a consistent quality and style in your posts, which is crucial for brand recognition and customer engagement. When you're not rushing to create posts daily, you have more time to consider your overall strategy and how each post fits into your larger marketing goals.

Leveraging Automation Tools

Automation can be a game-changer in managing your social media presence. Tools like Sprout Social, Buffer, and Hootsuite allow you to schedule posts, interact with followers, and monitor your social media feeds all from one dashboard. These tools can save you a significant amount of time by automating routine tasks, allowing you to focus more on what really matters—growing your business and engaging with customers.

Moreover, many of these tools come with analytics features that help you track the performance of your posts. Understanding what content resonates with your audience can help you refine your strategy and invest more in the types of posts that generate engagement, leads, and conversions.

Content Themes and Series

Consider developing themes or series to keep your audience engaged and make content creation easier. This approach can help turn a sprawling, unfocused social media feed into a cohesive, engaging narrative that pulls followers along from post to post. For example, if you're a plumber, you might have a weekly series on quick plumbing fixes homeowners can do themselves or a monthly deep-dive into different types of home plumbing systems.

Themes and series not only make it easier for you to plan and create content, but they also give your audience something to look forward to, increasing the likelihood they'll keep coming back. Additionally, this method can position you as an authority in your field, building trust and credibility with your audience.

Do not waste time trying to reinvent the wheel. Choose a few core pieces of content and create them from a different perspective each week. Here are the ten pillars of content you need in your portfolio:

1. **Product/Service Showcase**: Highlight the features and benefits of your products or service in action. Show how they solve a problem or enhance the lives of your customers.

2. **Behind-the-Scenes**: Offer a glimpse into the inner workings of your business. Show your team at work, share your creative process, or take viewers on a workspace tour.

3. **Customer Testimonials**: Showcase satisfied customers sharing their positive experiences with your products or services. Authentic testimonials can build trust and

credibility.

4. **Tutorials or How-To Guides**: Share valuable knowledge or skills related to your industry. Teach your audience something new and position yourself as an expert in your field.

5. **Q&A Sessions**: Host live or recorded question-and-answer sessions where you address common questions from your audience. This helps build rapport and allows you to provide valuable insights.

6. **User-Generated Content**: Share content your customers create using your products or services. This not only showcases your offerings but also encourages engagement and loyalty.

7. **Special Offers or Promotions**: Create videos to announce exclusive deals, discounts, or promotions. Use compelling visuals and clear calls to action to drive conversions.

8. **Company Culture**: Highlight your company culture to showcase your brand's personality and values. Share fun team activities, celebrations, or community involvement.

9. **Educational Content**: Share informative content related to your industry or niche. This could include indus-

try trends, tips, or valuable insights for your audience.

10. **Storytelling**: Share stories that resonate with your audience and reflect your brand's values. These could be success stories, anecdotes from your journey as a business owner, or stories about how your products have made a difference in people's lives.

Delegating and Outsourcing

As your business grows, you might find delegating or outsourcing some of your social media tasks worthwhile. However convenient this may sound, the pitfall is that most business owners hire a social media manager and expect all of the strategy development and problem-solving to fall to this person. That's insanity! You cannot expect an outsourced social media manager to know your business as well as you do nor be able to make the correct adjustments to your social media strategy that stay aligned with your overall goals. So, before you try to cut corners and outsource any aspect of your marketing, you must have the following in place:

- a written social media strategy

- clearly defined KPIs and goals

- a descriptive brand guide with examples of tone, language and style

- a content calendar built out

- scheduled times for reviewing content and conveying feedback

I've created that follow-along guide so you will have a digital file with all of this included. If you're filling it out as you read, you will have a full-scope marketing strategy in-hand when you complete this book. If you haven't already, snag yours at jrhoadesconsultinggroup.com/digitalmarketingworkbook.

When you have created and posted enough of your own content, meaning a minimum of several hundred posts across platforms, getting expert help can enhance the quality of your content and the effectiveness of your social media strategies.

By using content calendars, batching your content creation, leveraging themes and automation tools, and considering outsourcing, you can maintain a consistent and effective social media presence without it needing to become a second job. These strategies are designed to fit into your busy schedule, ensuring your social media efforts drive value and support your business goals efficiently.

5.2 Engaging With Your Audience Without Spending Your Life Online

As a small business owner, every minute counts, and it's crucial to find a balance that keeps your social media presence active and engaging without it consuming all your personal time. Here are some practical tips on how to keep the digital dialogue flowing with your audience while also keeping your free time free.

Firstly, consider the power of automated tools designed to streamline social engagement. Tools like Buffer or Hootsuite, for example, aren't just for scheduling posts. They can also help you manage interactions. You can set up alerts for when your business is mentioned or when there are comments on your posts, allowing you to respond quickly and efficiently. This kind of tool can be a lifesaver, ensuring that you stay responsive and engaged with your audience without needing to constantly check every notification. This responsive yet efficient approach means you can set aside specific times of the day to check in and engage rather than being on-call at all hours.

Another time-saving strategy is to create and use response templates for common queries or comments. If you find yourself answering the same questions about your services or business hours, having a set of pre-written, personalized responses can save you a significant amount of time. These templates can be customized on the fly to maintain a personal touch, so your audience doesn't feel like they're just talking to a robot. This method not only speeds up your response times but also helps in maintaining a consistent voice in your communications.

Building a sense of community among your followers can also lead to a more self-sustaining form of engagement. When your customers start to see your social media pages as forums where they can exchange ideas, share experiences, and even support each other, you'll find that not all the pressure to engage is on you. Encouraging user-generated content, such as asking customers to share photos of them using your product or participating in challenges, can foster this sense of community. This not only enhances engagement but also builds customer loyalty and helps create a more vibrant, interactive online presence.

Lastly, remember that being responsive does not mean being instantaneous. It is important to manage expectations about how quickly you can realistically respond to comments and queries. Making it clear when your audience can expect a response (for example, within 24 hours) helps manage your time and prevents customer frustration. This approach respects your time and customers' needs, balancing responsiveness with efficiency.

By implementing these strategies, you can maintain an active and engaging social media presence that drives your business forward without taking over your life. Each of these methods helps streamline your social media processes, ensuring that you spend your time online effectively and engage with your audience in a way that's both meaningful and manageable. This balance is key to maintaining your sanity and ensuring that your social interactions continue to contribute positively to your business's growth and success.

5.3 Paid vs. Organic Social Media Growth Strategies

Navigating the complexities of social media marketing can often feel like deciding between investing in high-quality tools for your trade or making do with what you've got and focusing on honing your skills. In social media terms, this translates into choosing between paid and organic growth strategies—each has its merits and pitfalls, and understanding these can significantly impact how you allocate your efforts and resources.

Understanding the Pros and Cons

Organic growth on social media is akin to relying on word-of-mouth in your local community; it's about building relationships and reputation over time. It involves creating content that resonates with your audience, engaging with followers, and optimizing your use of hashtags and keywords to increase your visibility and reach naturally. The major advantage here is cost—apart from your time, organic growth doesn't require a financial investment. However, the downside is that it can be slow, unpredictable, and heavily dependent on the ever-changing algorithms of the platforms.

On the flip side, paid social media strategies involve using paid ads to reach a broader audience. Platforms like Facebook, Instagram, and Twitter offer various advertising options tailored to different goals, whether it's boosting a post, promoting your page, or driving traffic to your website. The immediate benefit of paid strategies is visibility. You can reach a large number of people quickly, and you can target your ads to specific demographics, locations, and even interests, ensuring that your content is seen by those most likely to be interested in your services. The downside? Cost. Unlike organic strategies, you'll need to invest money, and there's always the risk that, if not managed well, it can lead to significant spending with little return if the ads are not optimized for conversion.

Budgeting for Paid Campaigns

Effectively managing your budget for paid campaigns requires a clear understanding of your goals and a keen eye on performance metrics. Start small; you don't need to pour thousands into Facebook ads right off the bat, but you should be prepared to do so if that's what is required to hit your goals. Start by setting a modest budget and run a few test campaigns to gauge what kind of messaging, imagery, and targeting yield the best results. This testing phase is crucial as it allows you to understand which aspects of your paid strategy are working and which aren't, enabling you to allocate more budget to the most effective tactics.

Moreover, consider the timing of your campaigns. For instance, if you run a seasonal business, like landscaping or holiday light installation, align your paid campaigns with these high-demand times to maximize your ROI. Additionally, keep a close eye on your cost-per-click or cost-per-acquisition; these metrics will tell you how much you are spending to gain one customer, helping you to decide whether your investment is justified.

Maximizing Organic Reach

To enhance your organic reach, focus on creating high-quality, engaging content that encourages interaction. Social media platforms favor content that generates engagement, such as comments, shares, and likes. Therefore, posts that prompt a response—like questions or polls—can perform better organically. Also, consistency is key in organic growth. Maintain a regular posting schedule to keep your audience engaged and to signal to social media algorithms that your page is active, which can help increase your content's visibility.

Another tactic is to leverage user-generated content. Encourage your customers to post about their experiences with your brand and to tag your business. This not only provides you with additional content that you can share, but it also increases your visibility and reach organically as friends of your customers see these posts.

Combining Paid and Organic Efforts

The most effective social media strategies often involve a mix of both paid and organic efforts. Use organic strategies to build and engage your base audience and establish a strong brand presence. This creates a solid foundation that enhances the effectiveness of your paid campaigns. Conversely, use paid strategies to amplify your best organic content, promote special offers, or boost posts that are performing well organically.

For instance, if a particular post is receiving a lot of organic engagement, putting some budget behind it to boost it can exponentially increase its reach and effectiveness. Similarly, insights from your paid campaigns can inform your organic content strategy. If certain messages or images perform well in ads, consider incorporating similar elements into your regular posts.

By understanding and balancing the strengths and weaknesses of both paid and organic growth strategies, you can create a holistic social media presence that not only reaches a wide audience but also engages and converts them effectively. This balanced approach ensures you are not overly reliant on any single method, providing a more stable and sustainable pathway to growing your business's online presence.

5.4 Tracking Your Social Media ROI

Understanding the return on investment (ROI) from your social media efforts is like keeping a scorecard in sports—it tells you what's working, what isn't, and where you should focus your energy to improve your game. It helps ensure that every hour and dollar you invest contributes to your overarching goal of growing your business and supporting your family.

Knowing the ROI of your social media activities isn't optional; it's a necessity if you're going to be successful with digital marketing.

Defining ROI for Social Media

To start, ROI in the context of social media is measured by how much value you get back from the resources you invest in your social media campaigns. This could be in terms of increased sales, more leads, enhanced customer engagement, or even improved brand awareness. Each business will have different objectives, and thus, ROI will look different for everyone. For instance, if your goal is to increase foot traffic in your store, your ROI might be measured by the number of customers who visit your shop after seeing a promotion on Facebook. If brand awareness is your aim, your ROI could be the number of shares or new followers on your social profiles.

To effectively measure ROI, you must set clear, measurable objectives before launching any social media campaign. These objectives should be directly tied to your business goals and as specific as possible. For example, rather than simply aiming to 'increase brand awareness,' set a goal to 'increase Instagram followers by 20% within three months'. Specific targets will guide your social media activities and provide clear benchmarks against which to measure your ROI.

Key Metrics to Monitor

The next step is to identify which metrics you need to monitor to evaluate your ROI effectively. These metrics will vary depending on your specific goals but generally include the following:

- **Engagement rates**: This includes likes, comments, shares, and overall interaction with your content. High engagement rates indicate that your content resonates well with your audience.

- **Conversion rates**: How many of the clicks on your social media posts result in a desired action, such as a purchase, a sign-up, or a download? This metric is crucial for understanding how effectively your social media campaigns drive tangible business results.

- **Reach and impressions**: These metrics tell how many people have seen your posts. While they don't measure engagement, they are useful for understanding the potential size of your audience.

- **Click-through rates (CTR)**: This measures how many people clicked on a link in your post. A higher CTR indicates your content is compelling enough to encourage further interaction.

Don't get caught in the trap of tracking every metric; you'll drive yourself crazy. The metrics listed above and your Key Performance Indicators (KPIs) that we discuss in the next chapter will be the only data you'll use to make decisions for your business.

Tools for Tracking and Analysis

Thankfully, you don't have to track these metrics manually. There are numerous tools available that can automate the tracking and analysis of your social media performance. Platforms like Google Analytics, Hootsuite, and Sprout Social offer comprehensive analytics to help you understand your social media ROI. These tools can provide detailed reports on your social media activities, showing which posts generate the most engagement, which platforms drive the most traffic to your website, and how your social media efforts translate into sales or other business outcomes.

Adjusting Strategies Based on Data

The real power of tracking your ROI lies in how you use this information to optimize your future social media strategies. By understanding what works and what doesn't, you can make informed decisions about how to allocate your resources and adjust your tactics to improve your results. For instance, if you find that Facebook ads have a higher conversion rate than NextDoor ads, you might reallocate more of your budget to Facebook.

Additionally, social media is dynamic, and audience preferences can change. Regularly reviewing the data allows you to stay adaptable and responsive to these changes, ensuring your social media strategy remains effective over time. It's about being proactive, not just reactive, using data to continuously refine and improve your approach to social media marketing.

In essence, tracking your social media ROI isn't just about justifying your marketing spend. It's about strategically investing in the activities that contribute most significantly to your business goals, ensuring that your efforts are not just fruitful, but cost-effective. By defining clear ROI metrics, utilizing the right tools for tracking and analysis, and being willing to adjust your strategy based on what the data tells you, you can maximize the impact of your social media efforts—turning posts, tweets, and shares into real business growth.

The insights and tactics discussed in this chapter are designed to help you navigate the complexities of social media marketing without it overwhelming your schedule or resources. As we transition into the next chapter, we'll focus more in-depth on paid advertising—what it is, how to use it, and how to maximize ROI.

This was a pretty heavy chapter with a lot of information that could be sending you into overdrive. If you haven't already done so, go download the free follow-along guide and take a few minutes to work on Section 4. It's better to practice this new skill while it's still fresh. You can download that guide at jrhoadesconsultinggroup.com/digitalmarketingworkbook.

Share Your Thoughts and Make an Impact

Your Review Can Help Others Small Business Owners Succeed

> "The best marketing strategy ever: CARE." - Gary Vaynerchuk

We all know how it feels to start something new, especially when it comes to mastering digital marketing for your business. The truth is, small business owners everywhere are eager to learn how to boost their online presence, attract customers, and scale their businesses. But sometimes, they just don't know where to begin.

That's where you come in.

By sharing your experience with *The Busy Entrepreneur's Guide To Digital Marketing*, you're not just leaving a review—you're giving another business owner the confidence to take that first step.

Your review could be the difference between someone struggling with confusing marketing strategies or finally finding the clarity they need to succeed. Imagine helping…

…one more business thrive in your community.

...one more entrepreneur grow their dream.

...one more family achieve stability.

...one more customer find the service they've been looking for.

...one more idea turn into reality.

Your feedback means the world to us and to those who are just starting their journey in digital marketing. It only takes a minute, but your review could make a lasting impact.

To share your thoughts, simply scan the QR code below and leave a review:

Thank you for taking the time to help others. Your kindness and generosity can spark the change that so many are looking for.

With gratitude,

Janessa Rhoades, Owner of Rhoades Consulting Group

6

Paid Advertising Essentials

Navigating the realm of paid advertising can feel like steering a ship through foggy waters for many small business owners. You know there's potential treasure out there—increased sales, more leads, greater visibility—but the route to getting there isn't always clear. This chapter will serve as your lighthouse, illuminating the essential metrics and strategies to effectively manage your paid advertising campaigns without needing a deep reservoir of marketing expertise or a hefty budget.

6.1 The Metrics You Actually Need To Know

Let's demystify some of the jargon starting with PPC, or Pay-Per-Click, a model of internet marketing in which you, the advertiser, pay a fee each time one of your ads is clicked. Essentially, it's a way of buying visits to your site rather than attempting to "earn" those visits organically. CPL, or Cost-Per-Lead, measures how cost-effective your marketing campaigns are when generating new leads for your business. Another crucial term is Return on Ad Spend (ROAS), which assesses the effectiveness of a digital advertising campaign. ROAS helps you understand the revenue your business earns for each dollar it spends on advertising.

For small businesses like yours, PPC can be a particularly cost-effective tool. It allows you to set a budget—whether that's $5 a day or $500—and only pay when someone clicks on your ad. This focus ensures your marketing budget is spent on potential customers, not just impressions or views.

Setting Up Your First Campaign

Launching your first PPC campaign might seem daunting, but it can be broken down into manageable steps. First, define the goal of your campaign. Are you looking to drive traffic to your website, generate new leads, or promote a specific product or sale? Once you have a clear goal, choose the platform that best suits your needs, whether that's Google Ads, Facebook Ads, or another platform. Each platform has its strengths, and the right one for you depends on where your customers are most likely to be found.

The next step is setting up your budget. Start small; you can always increase your budget later as you begin to see results. Most platforms offer incredibly detailed targeting options, allowing you to specify who sees your ads based on factors like location, age, interests, and more. Take advantage of these features to ensure that your target demographic sees your ads, maximizing the impact of every dollar spent.

Keyword Research for PPC

Keywords are the foundation of any PPC campaign, especially if you're using search advertising. They are the terms and phrases that users type into search engines when looking for the products or services you offer. Conducting thorough keyword research helps you understand what potential customers are searching for so you can tailor your ads to meet these queries.

Start by brainstorming the terms that are most relevant to your business. Tools like Google Keyword Planner can help you expand this list by suggesting related terms, showing you the search volume for each keyword, and the estimated cost to target them. Focus on keywords that are specific enough to attract highly qualified customers but broad enough that they generate a sufficient number of searches. For instance, if you own a plumbing business in Austin, targeting a keyword like "emergency plumber Austin" could be more effective than simply "plumber."

Measuring Success

To truly understand the effectiveness of your PPC campaigns, you need to track specific metrics that reflect your goals. Key metrics include:

- **Cost Per Lead (CPL):** This tells you how much you spend to acquire each lead. Tracking CPL helps ensure that the cost of acquiring a lead does not surpass the value of the lead for your business.

- **Number of Leads:** Tracks how many potential customers interact with your ads by completing an action like filling out a contact form. Your revenue goals will determine the number of leads you're aiming for.

- **Number of Appointments:** For service-based businesses, it's crucial to know how many of the leads turn into scheduled appointments. When it comes to cold internet traffic—meaning people who have found you strictly through your online ads—the goal is to convert 50% into appointments that show up.

- **Cost Per Appointment:** This measures the cost of securing each appointment through your PPC efforts. The goal is to keep your Cost Per Appointment at 40% of your Cost Per Conversion or lower.

- **Number of Conversions:** For the purpose of determining ROAS, a conversion is a sale of your primary service offering.

- **Cost Per Conversion:** Understanding how much you are spending to achieve each conversion helps assess the campaign's profitability. When trying to scale, your Cost Per Conversion should be one-third of the price of your primary service offering or lower.

- **Return on Ad Spend (ROAS):** This is the big-picture metric that shows the overall effectiveness of your advertising efforts in terms of monetary returns.

Monitoring these metrics provides actionable insights into what's working and what's not, allowing you to make informed decisions about adjusting your campaigns. Here's an example of how all of these metrics work together:

Let's say you're a plumber, your revenue goal next month is $30k, and your primary service costs $1000. Now, let's say for every 10 leads your business obtains, five of those turn into completed appointments, and for every five completed appointments you run, three will turn into conversion.

Based on this math, you must convert 30 sales, complete 50 appointments, and generate 100 leads.

If your CPL is $10, you can estimate spending $1000 to generate 100 leads.

Your Cost Per Appointment should be no higher than $133, and your Cost Per Conversion should be no higher than $330.

Run the same example for your revenue goals; these will be your Key Performance Indicators (KPIs), benchmarks on which you will measure progress.

You analyze the actual numbers generated over that time frame to determine your actual cost per appointment, cost per conversion, and ROAS.

For example, if you spent $1500 on advertising, generated 100 leads, ran 25 appointments, converted ten sales, and collected $8k from new acquisitions (this will include revenue from all financing options), your metrics would be as follows:

Actual Cost Per Appointment: $60 (within KPI)

Actual Cost Per Conversion: $150 (within KPI)

ROAS: 5X

I know you have a lot of questions about the math, so the image on the next page walks you through all of that.

# of Leads Total	Ad Spend	Cost Per Lead	Total Revenue Collected
# of leads generated for organic sources, walk ins, and paid advertising	Amount spent on paid advertising, boosted posts, and marketing materials	amount spent / # of leads	Total revenue collected for the month

# of Opportunities	Opportunity Percentage	Acceptable Cost Per Opportunity	Actual Cost Per Opportunity
# of sales appointments actually run	# of opportunities/ # of leads	amount you can spend on an opportunity to be break even	actual ammount spent per opportunity

# of Conversions Total	Conversion Percentage	Acceptable Cost Per Conversion	Actual Cost Per Conversion
# of sales closed on your average or biggest ticket package	# of conversions / # of opportunities	amount you can spend on a close to be break even (can be up to but no greater than 33% of total package price)	actual amount spent per close

Average Package Value	New Customer Revenue Collected	Total Contracted	ROAS
price of your average or biggest package	Total ammount collected from new customers you've acquired	Total ammount contracted for services sold	Revenue collected from new clients this month/ ad spend this month

An explanation of how to calculate your metrics and KPIs.

# of Leads Total	Ad Spend	Cost Per Lead	Total Revenue Collected
100	$1,500.00	$15.00	$33,579

# of Opportunities	Opportunity Percentage	Acceptable Cost Per Opportunity	Actual Cost Per Opportunity
40	40%	$132.00	$37.50

# of Conversions Total	Conversion Percentage	Acceptable Cost Per Conversion	Actual Cost Per Conversion
10	25.00%	$330.00	$150.00

Average Package Value	New Customer Revenue Collected	Total Contracted	ROAS
1000	$8,000.00	$10,000.00	5

This table shows you the calculations for the example above.

A quick analysis of these numbers will show you the exact things you need to work in your business over the next 30 days. In this example, we see that we hit our lead goal, but our conversion rate of turning those leads into showed appointments was 25% when our goal was 40%. Working on our follow up procedures or the quality of our phone calls would be the first area of focus.

Because the ROAS was so great, the next strategic move would be to increase ad spend.

One additional thing to remember is to use the broader numbers in the business. For example, if 15 of those 100 leads came from organic social media or word-of-mouth referrals, you'll still use the whole number. If you piece every data point out, you will do nothing but sift through data. Plus, someone may hear about your services from a neighbor, go to Google to check out your reviews, and ultimately click on your ad to become a lead; marketing is so intertwined that you may never truly know which piece it was that got that person to take action.

Lastly, anything above a 3X ROAS on paid advertising is considered "good." Think about it like putting $1 into an ATM and getting $3 back. If your ROAS is higher than 3X and you have big revenue goals, you should put more money into your paid ads because you're ready to scale.

Only by understanding and tracking these essential metrics can you effectively manage your ad campaigns, making sure that every dollar spent is an investment in growing your business. This strategic approach not only helps optimize your ad spend but also ensures that your advertising efforts contribute to tangible business outcomes, aligning with your overall goal of growth.

There's a digital copy of this table with the formulas built in that you can use for your own business in the follow-along workbook. You can find that at:

jrhoadesconsultinggroup.com/digitalmarketingworkbook.

6.2 Crafting Winning Ads on a Budget

Navigating the waters of paid advertising can seem daunting, especially when terms like 'click-through rates' and 'conversion optimization' start flying around. But let's cut through all the noise. The core objective of your paid advertising is straightforward: to generate leads. This means you need to be on the platforms where your ideal clients hang out, craft messages that hit home with them, and make it as easy as possible for them to connect with your business.

Though most, if not all, of the social media platforms give you the ability to communicate with your leads directly on the platform, the most effective way to capture lead data is by utilizing Customer Relationship Management (CRM) systems that feature landing pages specifically designed for this purpose. Simply put, your ad would lead a prospect to your landing page, and your landing page would capture their contact info. I will provide you more details on great landing pages in the next chapter. For now, let's stay focused on the paid ads part.

There are a handful of core components that make engaging and effective ads. Creating compelling ad copy is critical in catching the eye of potential customers. Your words must resonate with your audience, addressing their needs or solving their problems, encouraging them to click through to learn more. You've already done a ton of work to hone your buyer persona, so use the language from that exercise. Additionally, choose the promotion you think would resonate best to get them to stop scrolling and click on your ad. Remember, the key is to be clear and concise. You want your message to be understood quickly as social media users scroll through their feeds.

The core components of an effective paid ad are:

- **Ad Creative:** This includes the images or videos used in the ad.

- **Ad Copy:** The text used in the ad, including the headline, primary text, and call-to-action (CTA) button.

- **Ad Format:** Experiment with different ad formats, such as carousel ads, single image ads, video ads, or slideshow ads.

- **Headline:** Experiment with different headlines to see which attracts more clicks and engagement.

- **Promotion:** An enticing promotion gives people a reason to click on your ad.

- **Call to Action (CTA):** Testing different CTAs to see which ones drive more conversions and actions from your audience.

- **Audience Targeting:** This involves adjusting the demographic, interest, or behavioral targeting criteria to reach different segments of your audience.

The following image is an example of a Facebook ad for a med spa. I've tried to highlight the good things happening in this ad so you can see how they all work together.

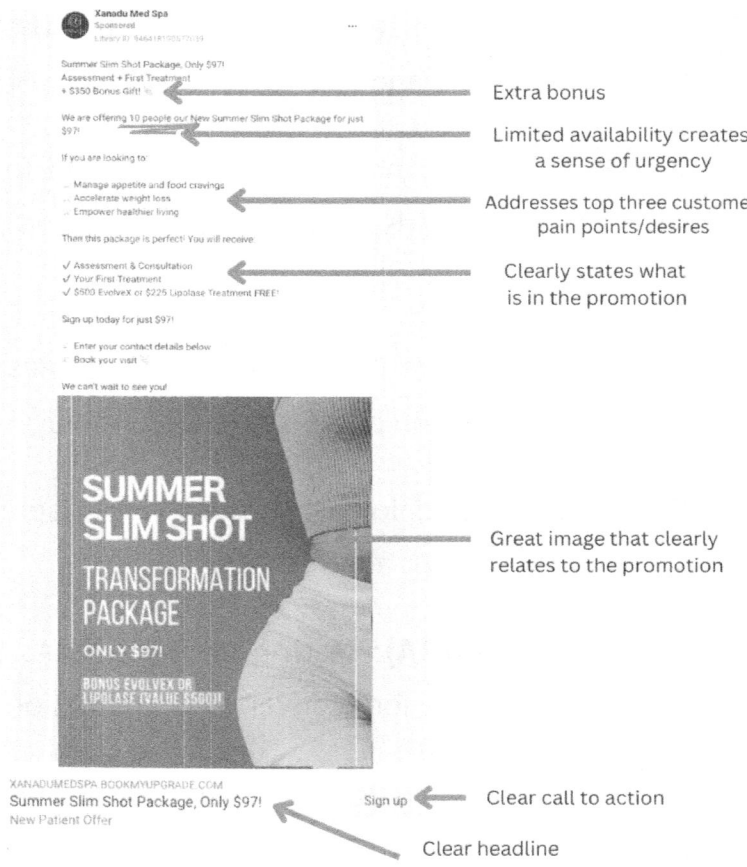

An example of a great Facebook ad

When starting out, you'll need to A/B test your ads to fine-tune them. By tweaking elements of your ad, like the headline or the image, and running these variations simultaneously, you can see which resonates more with your audience. The key here is to change one variable at a time so you know what changes are actually effective. Sometimes, a stunning graphic created in Canva can perform better than a video, or longer and more authentic ad copy can get more clicks than short copy that just focuses on the promotion. This continuous learning process helps craft future campaigns that are even more targeted and effective, ensuring that your ad budget is used as efficiently as possible. Remember, the goal of your advertising is not just to reach as many people as possible but to reach the right people—those who are most likely to become your customers.

If you've never run paid ads before, I know your biggest question is, "how much do I spend?" There are so many factors that lead to answering this, but my simplest answer would be, "As much as you need to spend to hit your goals."

As you start out, you will have to actively manage your advertising budget to ensure that your spending translates into tangible results. This involves not just setting a budget, typically a daily spend budget, but tweaking it based on the performance of your ads. A good rule of thumb is to run an ad for 72 hours before implementing any changes. From there, if the ad is within KPI let it run and gather more data; if it's significantly outside KPI, kill it – i.e. shut it off. Scale your spending as you see which ads are performing well. This iterative process allows you to optimize your expenditure and ensure the best possible ROAS.

By focusing on creating targeted, compelling, and visually appealing ads, and by managing your budget carefully, you can make the most of your advertising spend, driving leads and ultimately, sales, even on a tight budget. This **strategic** approach ensures that every dollar you spend is an investment towards growing your business, helping you achieve your ultimate goal of providing a comfortable life for your family through the success of your business.

6.3 A Primer on Building Social Media Ads

Tapping into the power of local Pay-Per-Click (PPC) and social media ads can significantly amplify your business's visibility in your locality. Here's a rundown of what works best on each of the major advertising platforms you'll use for advertising your business locally.

Facebook

- **Creative**: Visually appealing images or videos that showcase your services in action and clearly show your promotion.

- **Copy**: Short, engaging copy that highlights key benefits and includes a clear call to action.

- **Demographic Targeting**: Extensive targeting options based on demographics, interests, behaviors, and connections.

- **Alternative Targeting Functions**: Facebook offers advanced targeting options such as lookalike audiences, custom audiences, and engagement targeting. Beneficial if you already have a database of customers you can use as a foundation for targeting

- **Nuances**: Ads may initially enter a learning phase where Facebook's algorithm optimizes delivery, so patience is key.

- **Budgets**: Starting budgets can range from $5 to $20 per day, with adjustments based on campaign performance.

- **Analytics**: Tracks metrics such as reach, engagement, CPL, and conversions.

Instagram

- **Creative**: High-quality images or videos that align with the visual aesthetic of the platform, with attention-grabbing visuals and minimal text overlay.

- **Copy**: Concise yet compelling captions that complement the visual content and encourage engagement.

- **Demographic Targeting**: Leveraging Facebook's targeting capabilities with a focus on interests and behaviors relevant to Instagram users.

- **Alternative Targeting Functions**: Utilize Instagram-specific targeting options such as hashtag targeting and Instagram shopping tags.

- **Nuances**: Stories ads are a popular format for Instagram, offering immersive, full-screen experiences for users.

- **Budgets**: Similar to Facebook, starting budgets can range from $5 to $20 per day, with adjustments based on performance.

- **Analytics**: Monitors metrics such as likes, comments, shares, and website visits.

Google Ads

- **Creative**: Text-based ads with compelling headlines and descriptions accompanied by relevant keywords.

- **Copy**: Concise yet informative ad copy that includes keywords, your promotion, and a strong call to action.

- **Demographic Targeting**: Targeting options include location-based targeting, device targeting, and audience targeting based on demographics, interests, and behaviors.

- **Alternative Targeting Functions**: Google Ads offers advanced targeting options such as remarketing, similar audiences, and in-market audiences.

- **Nuances**: Optimize campaigns for local searches by including location extensions and leveraging Google My Business.

- **Budgets**: Budgets vary depending on keyword competitiveness and target location but typically range from $500 to $2000 per month.

- **Analytics**: Monitor key metrics such as click-through rate (CTR), conversion rate, and cost per acquisition (CPA) to assess campaign performance.

NextDoor

- **Creative**: High-quality images showcasing your services, preferably in a square format for optimal display.

- **Copy**: Short, concise copy that highlights the value proposition and your promotion and includes a clear call to action.

- **Demographic Targeting**: Targeting options include location-based targeting to reach users in specific neighborhoods or zip codes.

- **Alternative Targeting Functions**: NextDoor offers targeting based on interests, household income, and home ownership status.

- **Nuances**: Engage with the community by participating in discussions and providing valuable insights to establish credibility.

- **Budgets**: Depending on the size of the target area, budgets can range from $50 to $200 per campaign.

- **Analytics**: Track metrics such as impressions, clicks, and conversions.

TikTok

- **Creative**: Entertaining and authentic videos that capture the attention of the audience, leveraging popular trends and music.

- **Copy**: Short, catchy captions that complement the video content and encourage interaction.

- **Demographic Targeting**: Limited targeting options compared to other platforms, with focus on age, gender, location, and interests.

- **Alternative Targeting Functions**: Utilize TikTok's unique ad formats such as branded hashtag challenges, branded effects, and in-feed ads.

- **Nuances**: Embrace the platform's creative culture and participate in trending challenges to maximize engagement.

- **Budgets**: Starting budgets can range from $50 to $200 per campaign, with adjustments based on campaign objectives and performance.

- **Analytics**: Monitors metrics such as views, likes, shares, and click-through rate (CTR).

YouTube

- **Creative**: Engaging video content that captures viewers' attention within the first few seconds, featuring high-quality visuals and clear audio.

- **Copy**: Concise video titles and descriptions that accurately describe the content and include relevant keywords for search optimization.

- **Demographic Targeting**: YouTube offers targeting options based on demographics, interests, and viewing behavior, allowing advertisers to reach specific audience segments.

- **Alternative Targeting Functions**: Utilize advanced targeting options such as affinity audiences, custom intent audiences, and video remarketing to refine targeting.

- **Nuances**: YouTube ads come in various formats, including skippable in-stream ads, non-skippable in-stream ads, video discovery ads, and bumper ads, each with its own targeting and pricing options.

- **Budgets**: Starting budgets can range from $10 to $50 per day, depending on campaign objectives and targeting options selected.

- **Analytics**: Monitors key metrics such as views, watch time, engagement rate, and conversion rate.

Twitter

- **Creative**: Eye-catching visuals or videos that stand out in users' feeds, accompanied by concise and engaging copy that sparks curiosity or provokes action.

- **Copy**: Short, punchy tweets with clear calls to action (CTAs) and relevant hashtags to increase visibility and engagement.

- **Demographic Targeting**: Twitter offers targeting options based on interests, demographics, behavior, and keywords, allowing advertisers to reach specific audiences.

- **Alternative Targeting Functions**: Utilize features such as Tailored Audiences, which allow you to target users who have interacted with your website or app, and Twitter Lists, which enable targeting based on specific user lists.

- **Nuances**: Keep in mind that Twitter is a fast-paced platform where trends and conversations evolve rapidly, so staying up-to-date with current events and engaging with trending topics can boost ad performance.

- **Budgets**: Starting budgets can range from $10 to $100 per day, depending on campaign objectives and targeting options selected.

- **Analytics**: Monitors metrics such as impressions, engagement rate, link clicks, and conversions.

LinkedIn

- **Creative**: Professional and visually appealing imagery or videos that convey the brand's message effectively, accompanied by clear and compelling ad copy that resonates with LinkedIn's professional audience.

- **Copy**: Longer-form ad copy that provides detailed information about products or services, addressing pain points and offering solutions, with a strong call to action (CTA) to encourage clicks or conversions.

- **Demographic Targeting**: LinkedIn offers precise targeting options based on job title, industry, company size, seniority, and more, allowing advertisers to reach specific professionals and decision-makers.

- **Alternative Targeting Functions**: Take advantage of features such as Matched Audiences, which allow you to retarget website visitors or upload email lists for custom audience targeting, and Account-Based Marketing (ABM) for targeting specific companies.

- **Nuances**: LinkedIn is a platform for professional networking and B2B connections, so ad content should be tailored to appeal to a professional audience and focus on industry-specific pain points and solutions.

- **Budgets**: Starting budgets can range from $10 to $50 per day for sponsored content or text ads, and higher budgets may be required for sponsored InMail campaigns or dynamic ads.

- **Analytics**: Tracks metrics such as impressions, click-through rate (CTR), engagement rate, and conversion rate.

6.4 Local Advertising Strategies That Work

When you're running a local brick-and-mortar business, your community isn't just your neighborhood; it's your customer base. This is where local advertising comes into its own, offering distinct advantages by allowing you to connect directly with a highly targeted audience right on your doorstep. The beauty of local advertising lies in its ability to foster a deeper connection between your business and the community you serve. This isn't about casting a wide net but about fishing in a well-stocked pond where every nibble has a higher chance of turning into a catch.

Local advertising excels in building brand awareness within the community, supporting local loyalty, and driving foot traffic—key ingredients for the sustenance and growth of any small business. When people see your business actively engaging within the local scene, whether through ads, local events, or community programs, it creates a sense of familiarity and trust. This is crucial because when customers decide where to shop or which services to use, they're more likely to choose a business they recognize and feel connected to.

Leveraging Local Directories and Platforms

Beyond PPC and social media, local directories like Yelp and Google My Business can be invaluable for local advertising.

These platforms are often the first place locals or visitors go to find services or businesses in their area. Ensuring your business is listed and actively managed on these directories is crucial. It's about more than just having your name and number out there. It's about making a good impression right off the bat.

Make sure your profiles are complete with up-to-date information, photos of your business, and any unique selling points that set you apart. Encourage happy customers to leave positive reviews and respond professionally to any negative ones, showing that you value customer feedback and are committed to improving service. These actions not only enhance your visibility but also build your reputation within the community, making potential customers more likely to choose you over competitors.

Creative Local Advertising Ideas

Finally, think outside the digital box when it comes to local advertising. Participating in or even hosting community events can significantly boost your local profile. Whether it's a neighborhood fair, a charity run, or a local festival, these events are opportunities to showcase your business to a captive audience. These activities increase your visibility and embed your business in the local community's consciousness.

Collaborations with other local businesses can also be a win-win for local advertising. For instance, you could partner with a nearby cafe to offer discounts to each other's customers or run a joint contest. These collaborations can double your exposure, reaching a broader yet still targeted audience. Plus, they deepen your roots in the local business community, which can lead to more opportunities and enhanced local support.

Through these strategies, local advertising can become a cornerstone of your marketing efforts, driving both growth and community engagement. By focusing on targeted local PPC and social media ads, making the most of local directories, and getting involved in community events and collaborations, you're not just advertising your business but making it a valued part of the local landscape. This approach doesn't just capture immediate sales; it builds a foundation of local loyalty and support to sustain your business long-term.

As we wrap up this chapter on paid advertising, remember that diving into paid advertising is not about instant mastery or perfect campaigns from the outset. It's about strategic experiments, continual learning, and adjustments that align with your business goals. Digital advertising platforms change fast so be ready to adjust quickly. In the next chapter, we'll explore the next crucial aspect of digital marketing — Search Engine Optimization.

7

SEO for the Local Market

Imagine you're the go-to person in your town for whatever service you provide, be it plumbing, carpentry, or boutique retail. Now, what if you could replicate that trust and recognition in the digital world? That's where local SEO comes into play. It's like being recommended by a friend to everyone in town who searches for your services online. In this bustling online marketplace, local SEO ensures your business stands out when and where it matters most—right in your own backyard.

7.1 Local SEO: A Primer for Small Business Owners

Local SEO (Search Engine Optimization) isn't just another buzzword; it's a crucial strategy that helps your business become more visible in local search results on Google and other search engines. Why does this matter? Because local search is often what drives foot traffic to brick-and-mortar businesses. When someone in your area searches for "best electrician near me" or "emergency plumber," you want your business to appear in the top results. This kind of visibility can dramatically increase your chances of that searcher becoming a customer. Local SEO involves optimizing your online presence to attract more business from relevant local searches. These searches take place on all major search engines, but for simplicity, we'll focus on Google, the largest and most used search engine.

Keywords for Local SEO

Choosing the right keywords is like picking the correct type of bait for the fish you want to catch. For local SEO, this means focusing on search terms that include local names or landmarks alongside your business offerings. Start by brainstorming a list of keywords that describe your business, then localize these keywords by adding the names of your city, neighborhood, or other local identifiers.

Here are the top keywords to use when it comes to local SEO:

1. [Service] + "Near me"

2. [Service] + [Location]

3. "Best [Service] in [Location]"

4. [Service] + "Nearby"

5. [Service] + "Open Now"

6. "Affordable [Service] [Location]"

7. [Service] + "Deals" or "Discounts"

8. "Emergency [Service] [Location]"

9. [Service] + "Appointment"

10. "Local Events" or "Things to Do" + [Location]

Tools like Google's Keyword Planner can help you expand this list by suggesting additional keywords based on local search trends. This tool also provides data on how often these terms are searched, giving you insight into the demand for your services in your area.

Use the following ChatGPT prompt to develop a list of relevant keywords for your business and location:

> I'm planning to run ads for a [your business type] in [your city], [your state]. Can you help me identify the top keywords related to this niche? I'm looking for keywords that potential patients might use when searching for [your niche] services in this area. Please provide a mix of general [your niche] keywords and those specific to [your location].

Additional ChatGPT prompts are included in the follow along guide. These initial prompts are for idea generation; use your common sense and trade expertise to finesse the prompt to get the best results possible. You can find your free copy at: jrhoadesconsultinggroup.com/digitalmarketingworbook.

The Role of Local Content

Content that resonates with a local audience can significantly boost your local search rankings. This means creating content that's not only relevant to your business but also to your local community. Including local keywords naturally within this content can help you rank higher in search results. Additionally, regularly updating your blog with local news or events can keep your content fresh and engaging, encouraging more visits to your site. Participating in or sponsoring local events and then featuring these activities on your social media or blog is also beneficial. This not only strengthens your community ties but also enhances your local relevance, which is favored by search engines.

Local SEO Checklist

To ensure you're covering all bases in local SEO, here's a quick checklist:

- **NAP Consistency:** NAP stands for Name, Address, and Phone Number. Make sure your business's NAP is consistent across all online platforms, from your website to your social media profiles and especially in local business directories.

- **Local Keywords:** Use local keywords strategically in your website's meta tags, headings, and throughout your content.

- **Engage with Local Communities:** Actively engage on social media with local customers and participate in community events. Share updates, participate in local conversations, and connect with other local businesses.

- **Optimize for Mobile:** Ensure your website is mobile-friendly. Most local searches are performed on mobile devices, and a mobile-optimized site provides a better user experience, encouraging more engagement and conversions.

By implementing these local SEO strategies, you're not just boosting your visibility in search results; you're laying down digital roots in your community. This helps attract more local customers and builds a long-term relationship with the community around your business, fostering loyalty that can sustain your business through changing times. Remember, local SEO is not a one-off task but an ongoing strategy that needs nurturing and adaptation as your business and community evolve.

7.2 Optimizing Your Google My Business Listing

Setting up and claiming your Google My Business (GMB) listing is akin to planting your business's flag on the digital map. It's a crucial step, especially for local businesses like yours, as it significantly boosts your visibility on Google's services, including Maps and Search. To get started, head to the Google My Business website and search for your business name. There's a chance it already exists, and if so, you'll need to claim it. If not, you can easily add it by entering your business details. The verification process typically involves Google sending a postcard with a verification code to your business address. This step is vital as it confirms the authenticity of your business location.

Once your business is verified, it's time to optimize your profile. This goes beyond just filling in the basics; it's about making your GMB listing a comprehensive resource for potential customers. Start with ensuring that your business name, address, and phone number are correct and consistent with those listed on your website and other online platforms. This consistency helps Google trust the validity of your business, which can improve your search ranking. Next, write a compelling business description highlighting what makes your service unique. This is your chance to tell your business's story in a way that resonates with potential customers and includes keywords that help you rank for relevant local searches.

Photos play a pivotal role in optimizing your GMB listing. Businesses with photos see significantly more clicks to their websites and requests for directions. However, don't just upload any photos; ensure they are high-quality images that represent your business well. Include pictures of your premises, your team at work, and before-and-after photos of your projects, if applicable. These images give potential customers a better sense of what to expect and can be the deciding factor in choosing your business over a competitor.

Encouraging customers to leave reviews on your GMB listing is another crucial element of local SEO. Reviews not only improve your business's credibility but also boost its visibility in search results. Reach out to satisfied customers and kindly ask them to share their experiences. You might do this via a follow-up email, a text message, or even in person after a service has been completed. Make the process as easy as possible by providing a direct link to where they can leave their review. As previously mentioned, it's important to regularly monitor and respond to reviews, regardless of whether they are positive or negative. A thoughtful response to a review shows that you value customer feedback and are committed to improving service quality, which can encourage more customers to choose your service.

Google My Business also offers features like Posts and Q&A, which provide additional ways to engage with potential customers. GMB Posts are updates you can create to promote events, offers, or news about your business. These posts appear in your GMB profile and in local search results, giving you a direct way to communicate with local customers and keep them updated. The Q&A feature allows people to ask questions about your business directly on your GMB listing. It's important to monitor and respond to these questions promptly and accurately, as other potential customers can see this information.

By taking full advantage of the features offered by Google My Business, you optimize your local SEO efforts and improve your visibility in local search results. This helps potential customers find you more easily and provides valuable information that can influence their decision to use your services. Remember, your Google My Business listing is often the first impression potential customers will have of your business, so make it count.

7.3 Building Local Links: A How-To Guide

If you think of your website as your digital storefront, then local backlinks are like the roads that lead customers right to your door. Just as a well-placed sign on a busy street can bring a steady stream of traffic into your shop, a strategically placed backlink on a reputable local website can drive significant traffic to your online presence. These links are essential because they tell search engines that other community members recognize and recommend a local business. This kind of endorsement can significantly boost your site's credibility and ranking in local search results, making it easier for potential customers to find you when searching for the services you offer.

Acquiring these local backlinks, however, requires a thoughtful approach. One effective strategy is to build partnerships with other local businesses that complement rather than compete with your services. For instance, if you run a wedding photography business, partnering with local florists or event venues can be beneficial. You can agree to feature each other's services on your blogs or websites, which not only provides valuable content for your customers but also creates a network of backlinks that bolsters your local SEO. Another avenue for building backlinks is through local business directories. Ensure your business is listed in all relevant online directories, and you're already on your way to building a solid backlink profile.

Participation in community events offers another excellent opportunity for local link-building. Whether it's sponsoring a local sports team, participating in charity events, or hosting a community workshop, these activities can generate news and interest, leading to mentions and links from local media outlets, event pages, and blogs. Make sure to leverage every event by asking organizers to include a link to your website on their event page or by creating engaging content about the event that local news outlets might pick up and link back to.

However, there are certain dos and don'ts you should keep in mind when it comes to local link building. Always prioritize quality over quantity. A few well-placed links from respected local sources are far more valuable than numerous links from poorly regarded websites. Be wary of any service offering to sell you a package of links; these are often low-quality and can do more harm than good to your SEO efforts. Instead, focus on building genuine relationships within your community that can naturally lead to high-quality backlinks.

Tracking and assessing the quality of your backlinks is crucial to ensure they benefit your local SEO efforts. Tools like Ahrefs or Moz can help you monitor your backlinks, checking their number and quality. Look for metrics like domain authority to gauge the credibility of linking sites. A link from a local business association's website with a high domain authority can be far more impactful than a dozen links from obscure blogs with little to no authority. Regular monitoring also helps you spot potentially harmful links quickly, allowing you to disavow them before they negatively impact your SEO.

By focusing on these strategies and maintaining a vigilant approach to monitoring your backlinks, you can enhance your local SEO significantly. Remember, each quality backlink is a vote of confidence in your business, improving your search engine ranking and your visibility and reputation within the local community. This, in turn, can lead to more foot traffic, more customers, and, ultimately, more growth for your business. So, consider each link as a crucial step in expanding your local digital footprint and invest in strategies that will create and sustain these connections.

7.4 On-Page SEO Tactics for Local Businesses

Optimizing your website's on-page elements is akin to setting up a welcoming storefront: it's about making your space inviting and easy to navigate for anyone who might stroll by. This starts with the nuts and bolts of your website—meta tags, descriptions, and headers—all tuned with a local SEO focus. Think of it like this: every time someone searches for services you offer in your area, your website's meta tags and descriptions are like signposts guiding them to your door. Ensuring these elements are optimized for local searches is crucial.

Start by tweaking your title tags and meta descriptions. These bits of HTML code in your website's header are critical because they tell search engines—and potential customers—what each page of your website is about. For local businesses, it's smart to include geographically specific terms. For instance, if you're a plumber in Naples, your title tag could be "Emergency Plumbing Services | Naples, FL - [Your Business Name]," and your meta description could elaborate with "Fast, reliable plumbing services in Naples. Available 24/7, ready to handle any emergency. Call now!" This clarity helps search engines rank you appropriately and makes your services clear to potential customers.

Headers are another essential piece of the puzzle. These are the H1, H2, H3 (and so on) tags used to structure content on your pages. Search engines pay attention to these because they often contain clues about the page's content. Ensure your headers include keywords relevant to your local business and reflect the language your customers might use when searching for your services. For instance, H1 could be "Top-Rated Naples Plumber" followed by H2s like "Leak Repairs and Plumbing Services in Naples" to keep reinforcing the local angle while staying relevant to what searchers are looking for.

Local Schema Markup

The concept of schema markup might not be something you're familiar with, but it's a powerful tool for local SEO. Schema markup is a code you put on your website to help search engines return more informative results for users. When it comes to local businesses, implementing localized schema markup can significantly enhance your visibility in search results.

Adding schema markup to your site could seem daunting, but it's essentially about telling search engines exactly what specific content on your site means. For instance, you can use LocalBusiness schema to highlight your business's name, address, phone number, and more. This not only helps search engines understand your business better but also increases the likelihood of your business appearing in rich snippets and the knowledge graph—prominent features in search results. Tools like Google's Structured Data Markup Helper can take you step by step through the process, making it easier to get started.

Mobile Optimization for Local Search

Nowadays, a mobile-optimized website isn't just nice to have; it's a necessity. With more and more users turning to their smartphones to find local services, having a website that's clunky and hard to navigate on a small screen can quickly drive potential customers away. The goal is to ensure that anyone visiting your site from a mobile device has as smooth an experience as they would on a desktop. This means fast load times, easy-to-navigate menus, and content that scales naturally to different screen sizes.

Google's Mobile-Friendly Test can tell you how well your site performs on mobile devices and offer suggestions for improvement. Remember, mobile optimization also affects your search rankings, as search engines prefer sites that provide a good user experience.

Improving Local Landing Pages

Your landing pages are where the rubber meets the road: they're where potential customers land after clicking on your ads or search engine listings. For local businesses, these pages need to be persuasive and clearly localized. Each landing page should focus on a specific service and location to improve its relevance in local searches. I repeat, do not convolute landing pages; if you run a dental office, one page will be for your teeth whitening services, while a separate landing page will be for your Invisalign promotion. Include location-specific information in your headers, title tags, and body content. For instance, if you're targeting customers in

Naples, mention landmarks, local events, or common issues relevant to the area to enhance the local connection.

Your call to action on these pages should also be clear and compelling. Whether you want visitors to fill out a contact form, call a phone number, or take advantage of a special offer, make sure this action is front and center. It's also wise to include testimonials or case studies that speak to the quality of your work and the satisfaction of your local customers. This builds trust and reinforces your standing in the local community.

Here are a few examples of great landing pages:

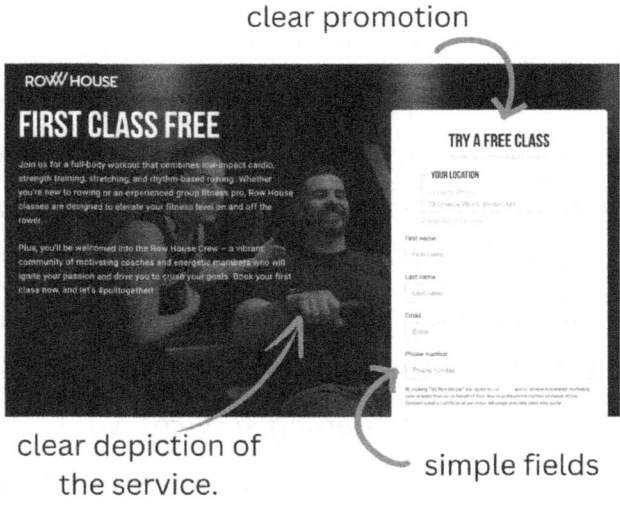

Example of a sleek and simple landing page.

Example of a great landing page with multiple contact options.

By focusing on these on-page SEO tactics and tips to make engaging landing pages, you can significantly enhance your website's visibility and appeal to potential local customers. Remember, the goal of local SEO isn't just to drive traffic—it's to convert that traffic into leads and customers who can help your business grow. As you implement these strategies, keep a close eye on your site's performance and be ready to tweak and adjust your approach based on what the data tells you. This proactive stance ensures your site continues to serve your business's goals and supports your growth in the competitive local marketplace.

7.5 Using Local Events to Boost Online Visibility

Participating in local events is like casting a wide net in a fully stocked pond—it's about amplifying your presence while forging strong connections with the community. When you host or join local events, you're not just a faceless business; you become a visible, active member of the community. This visibility is not only crucial for building trust and rapport with potential customers but also for boosting your local SEO efforts. Search engines prioritize businesses that are actively involved in their local scene because it signifies relevance and authenticity—crucial elements in local search rankings.

Consider the last community fair or local festival you attended. Now envision your business having a booth there, or better yet, being one of the event sponsors. Such involvement can significantly enhance your local visibility. But it doesn't end at the event itself. Leveraging social media to promote these events can extend your reach even further. Use your social media platforms to discuss the event before, during, and after it takes place. Share updates, post photos, and use event-specific hashtags to boost engagement. This not only demonstrates your active participation but also keeps your business in the minds of locals who follow the event online.

Moreover, consider listing your events in local online directories and event calendars, many of which are free to use. These platforms are often frequented by locals looking for things to do, providing another avenue for potential customers to discover your business. Ensuring your events are listed increases the chances of local attendees becoming customers as they associate your business with community activities they enjoy.

Creating content around local events is another powerful strategy to boost your online visibility. For instance, if you sponsor a local charity run, create a blog post about why supporting local causes is important for your business. Include photos from the event and maybe even a video recap or interviews with participants. Such content not only enriches your website but also serves as engaging material for your social media channels. This approach helps in painting your business as socially responsible and community-focused, traits that can endear you to local customers.

Tracking the impact of these activities on your SEO and overall online visibility is crucial. Use tools like Google Analytics to monitor how traffic to your site changes before, during, and after local events. Look at metrics like page views, user engagement, and how visitors find your site—whether through direct searches, social media, or links from other sites. This data can provide valuable insights into the effectiveness of your event-related marketing efforts, helping you fine-tune your strategies for future events.

By actively integrating local events into your marketing and

SEO strategy, you not only enhance your community presence but also strengthen your online visibility, making your business a well-known name both offline and online

As we wrap up this exploration of leveraging local events for enhancing online visibility, remember that your involvement in the community does more than just boost your SEO—it builds lasting relationships with local customers, fostering loyalty and trust. This chapter has equipped you with strategies to maximize your visibility through local events, create content that resonates with your community, and track the effectiveness of these efforts. As you move forward, continue to engage with your community both online and offline, using every event as an opportunity to showcase your business and deepen your local connections. These efforts not only enhance your immediate business prospects but also lay a foundation for sustained growth and community integration in the future.

8

Email Marketing Mastery

Think of email marketing as your business's heartbeat, consistently pumping your brand's message directly into the inboxes of potential and existing customers. It's personal, direct, and, when done right, incredibly effective. But before you can send out that first captivating email, you need a list of people to send it to. Building an email list from scratch might sound like a daunting task, especially when you're managing a bustling small business with no time to spare. Yet, with the right strategies and tools, you can start growing your email list today, turning casual website visitors into loyal customers.

8.1 Building Your Email List from Scratch

Don't panic if you literally have zero contacts on your business' email list. To build a list you need two things – a reason why people will sign up and a way for them to give you their contact information. That's it.

Opt-in Strategies

The foundation of building an effective email list lies in creating compelling opt-in strategies. An opt-in is a permission-based agreement from someone to receive email communications from you. This is crucial because the last thing you want is to be marked as spam, which can hurt your ability to reach inboxes. The most effective way to get people to opt-in is by offering them something of value in return. This could be a digital product like an eBook, a discount code, or access to exclusive tips that resonate with your audience's needs and interests. For example, if you run an automotive repair shop, you might offer a free downloadable checklist of "Top 5 DIY Car Maintenance Tips" in exchange for an email address. This not only gives potential customers a reason to give you their email but also establishes your expertise in the automotive field. Think about what you can offer to your audience, and ask for their email in return.

Landing Pages for List Building

Dedicated landing pages are powerful tools specifically designed to convert visitors into email subscribers. These pages focus solely on one call to action—signing up for your list. The key here is simplicity and clarity. Your landing page should clearly state what visitors will gain by subscribing, coupled with a simple form to collect their emails. Make sure the design of the page minimizes distractions; every element should encourage subscription. For instance, the use of contrasting colors for the signup button can make it stand out, and testimonials or trust signals near the form can boost credibility and coax visitors to subscribe.

Compliance and Permission

Navigating the legal landscape of email marketing is not just a necessity but a foundation of trust between you and your subscribers. Compliance with laws like the CAN-SPAM Act in the U.S. or General Data Protection Regulation (GDPR) in the EU ensure that your email marketing practices respect user privacy and are transparent. This means ensuring your signup forms have clear information on what subscribers should expect regarding email frequency and content type and, importantly, ensuring there is a straightforward way for them to unsubscribe if they choose. Most reputable email builder platforms will have embedded security measures, but it is your responsibility to ensure you follow federal laws and regulations here.

Promoting Your Signup Form

Visibility is key to growing your email list, so your signup form should be easy to find across all your online platforms. Embed the signup form on your website, either in the header, as a pop-up, or before the footer, ensuring it's visible on relevant pages without disrupting the user experience. Additionally, promote your email list on your social media platforms. Share posts about the benefits of subscribing to your list, or consider using paid ads targeted at your desired audience to increase reach and visibility. For instance, a local bakery might run a Facebook ad campaign targeting local customers with the lure of a weekly newsletter that includes exclusive recipes and discounts.

By implementing these strategies, you start turning the wheels of your email marketing machine—steadily growing a list of engaged subscribers ready to hear from you. With every new subscriber, you gain another opportunity to showcase your expertise, promote your services, and, ultimately, drive sales. Remember, the key to successful email marketing doesn't just lie in the size of your list but in the quality and engagement of the subscribers you attract.

8.2 Crafting Emails That Get Opened and Read

Crafting an email that not only gets opened but also read and acted upon can feel like threading a needle while wearing boxing gloves—tricky, to say the least, especially when you're competing with countless others for attention in your customers' inboxes. The key starts with the subject line; it's the first impression and, often, the make-or-break element for whether your email even gets a glance. To create subject lines that beckon a click, you need to stir curiosity, convey urgency, or offer something that feels personally relevant to the reader. Imagine receiving an email with the subject line, "Last Chance to Grab Your 25% Off!" or "Are You Making These HVAC Maintenance Mistakes?" Both lines serve different purposes: the first creates urgency with a time-sensitive offer, while the second piques curiosity with a question that hints at valuable information.

Moving beyond the subject line, the content of your email must hold the promise made at the door. This is where storytelling comes into play, a technique not just reserved for novelists. As a small business owner, your services or products have stories—problems they solve and the joys they bring. Share these stories in your emails. For instance, instead of just listing the features of a new product, tell a story about how it was developed in response to customer feedback, emphasizing the value proposition. What does this product do for them that no other product can? Every email should clearly communicate this "value" in a way that resonates with your audience's needs and desires.

Design also plays a critical role in how your email is received. A cluttered, visually overwhelming email can deter readers, even if the content is excellent. Keep your design clean and focused. Use visuals like images or videos wisely—they should enhance your message, not distract from it. Most importantly, ensure your emails are optimized for mobile devices. A significant portion of emails are opened on smartphones and tablets; an email that can't be easily read on these devices is likely to be deleted in seconds. Use responsive design templates that adapt to different screen sizes and test your emails across different devices before sending them out to your list.

Personalization is another strategy that can dramatically increase the effectiveness of your emails. With the data you gather from subscriber interactions and behaviors, you can tailor your messages so they speak directly to individual needs or interests. This doesn't just mean inserting a customer's first name into the email. It's about segmenting your email list based on observed preferences or behaviors and crafting messages that appeal to these segments. For example, if you notice a segment of your list frequently purchases parts for classic cars, tailor your content to discuss tips, products, and services relevant to classic car maintenance and restoration. Personalized emails show your subscribers that you understand and value their specific interests, which can increase engagement and loyalty.

By focusing on these key areas—compelling subject lines, engaging storytelling, clean and responsive design, and thoughtful personalization—you can transform your email marketing into a powerful tool to connect with customers and drive results. Each email becomes an opportunity to deepen relationships with your customers, enhance your brand's reputation, and, ultimately, drive conversions. Remember, successful email marketing is about continual learning and adaptation, always striving to better meet the needs and interests of your subscribers while achieving your business goals.

8.3 Automating Your Email Marketing for Efficiency

Imagine a world where your email marketing takes care of itself, where messages are timed perfectly without you having to lift a finger for each send. That's the power of email automation, a system designed to send out emails automatically based on specific triggers and schedules you set. This isn't just about saving time; it's about increasing the effectiveness of your communications by ensuring they reach the right people at the right time with the right message.

Email automation works by using a set of rules that trigger certain emails based on specific actions taken by your subscribers. For instance, when a new subscriber joins your email list, an automated welcome email can be sent to introduce your business and set the tone for future communications. This initial touchpoint is crucial; it not only starts building a relationship but also boosts engagement by providing valuable information right when the subscriber's interest is piqued.

Setting up these automated email series isn't as complex as it might sound. Most modern email marketing platforms offer user-friendly interfaces that guide you through setting up automated workflows. The key is to map out the customer journey and identify key interaction points where automated emails could be beneficial.

For instance, after a purchase, you might set up a series that thanks the customer, provides additional product usage tips, and invites them to follow your social media channels. Each of these steps involves different content but is part of a cohesive communication strategy designed to enhance customer satisfaction and deepen engagement.

In the following example, the email automation is triggered by the purchase of a product. The recipient receives an email immediately after purchase and then three additional emails that are spaced out over the course of six days.

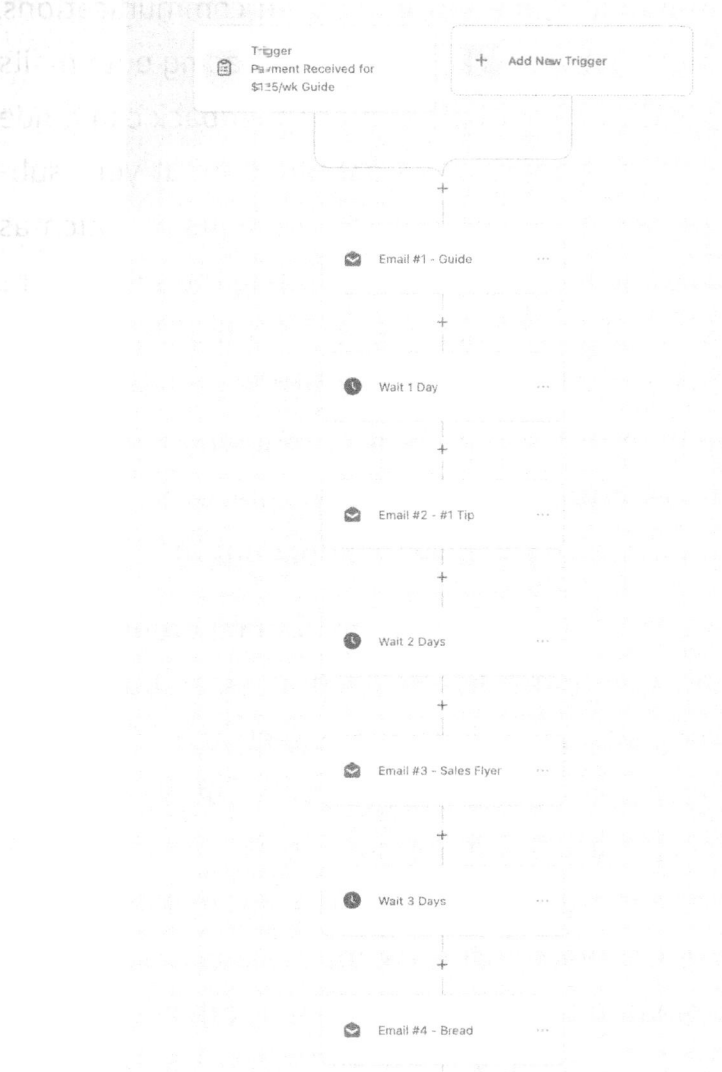

Example of a very simple email automation you can build in High Level.

When implementing email automation, there are several best practices to keep in mind. First, timing is crucial. You don't want to send too many emails too quickly, but you also don't want to let too much time lapse between communications. Finding the right balance is key. Typically, spacing out emails based on typical customer behavior and feedback can guide these decisions. Use data you've gathered about your subscribers to personalize the automated emails as much as possible. This could be as simple as including the subscriber's name in the email or as complex as tailoring the content based on their past behavior or purchase history. Also, keep an eye on frequency. It's important to regularly review your automation settings to ensure you are not overwhelming your subscribers, which can lead to higher unsubscribe rates.

In terms of tools and platforms, there are numerous options available that cater to the diverse needs of small businesses. Platforms like Mailchimp, Constant Contact, and Sendinblue not only offer robust automation features but also provide analytics tools to track the performance of your emails. These platforms are designed to be user-friendly, making it easy for someone without extensive technical skills to set up and manage automated campaigns. They also offer scalability, which means they can grow with your business as your marketing needs evolve. However, I again recommend a platform called High Level because it is a full-scope CRM that allows you to build landing pages, email and text your audience, and helps you manage your social media presence. Here's a code you can click or scan for a 14-day free trial:

Remember, this is an affiliate link and I get commissions for purchases made through this QR code.

By leveraging the power of email automation, you can streamline your marketing efforts, ensuring consistent and timely communication with your subscribers. This not only improves efficiency but also enhances the effectiveness of your email marketing by ensuring that your messages are relevant and timely. As you continue to refine your email marketing strategy, remember that automation is not set-it-and-forget-it; it requires ongoing tweaking and optimization based on subscriber behavior and feedback to maintain its effectiveness.

8.4 Measuring the Success of Your Email Campaigns

Understanding the effectiveness of your email marketing efforts is like checking the pulse of your campaigns—it tells you what's working, what isn't, and how you can improve. To really grasp the impact of your emails, you need to dive into the analytics. It starts with tracking the right metrics. Open rates, for instance, give you a clear picture of how many people are actually opening the emails you send. It directly reflects how compelling your subject lines are and whether your email times resonate with your audience. The average open rate for marketing and advertisement emails is around

17%. If you're seeing a significantly lower open rate, it's time to change the subject line.

Next, look at click-through rates (CTR), which measure how many people clicked on a link within your email. This metric is crucial because it goes beyond just opening an email to actually interacting with the content you've provided. The average CTR for advertising emails is between 1.5% and 2%. If your audience is opening your email and not clicking on what you have to offer, consider changing your call to action, making your offer more enticing, or reviewing your audience's pain points and needs to ensure your offer is relevant.

Conversion rates take your analysis a step further by showing how many of these interactions turned into actual sales or desired actions. If your CRM allows you to track this, this will be crucial information regarding the effectiveness of your email content and call-to-action placements.

Lastly, unsubscribe rates are equally important, though often overlooked. Average unsubscribe rates hover around .25%. If your unsubscribe rate is higher than average, you might be sending too many emails, they might be irrelevant to your audience, or your content is not aligning with subscriber expectations. Monitoring these rates closely allows you to safeguard your list's health and maintain a quality audience.

Analyzing this data helps you understand your subscribers' behavior and preferences. But raw data alone isn't enough—you need to interpret it to make informed decisions. For example, if you notice high open rates but low click-through rates, this could indicate that your messages are initially appealing but fail to keep readers engaged enough to take action. This insight directs you to enhance your email content or refine your calls-to-action.

A/B testing is your strategic tool in this refining process. By creating two versions of the same email with just one variation in elements like the subject line, content structure, or images and sending them to a small segment of your list, you can see which version performs better before rolling out to your entire list. This method not only optimizes your emails but also reduces the risk of larger campaign failures. The beauty of A/B testing lies in its ability to continuously improve the various components of your emails based on actual subscriber reactions rather than assumptions.

Utilizing these insights effectively demands applying them to refine and improve your email strategies continually. For instance, if A/B testing shows a clear preference for personalized subject lines, then adapting this approach across your campaigns could lead to consistently higher engagement rates. Similarly, if certain types of content consistently lead to higher conversions, consider prioritizing or producing more of that content type. This cyclical process of testing, learning, and applying helps keep your email campaigns fresh, relevant, and effective. A simple monthly review of your data is all it takes to optimize email campaigns.

By grounding your email marketing strategies in solid data analysis and responsive adaptations, you not only maximize the ROI of your campaigns but also cultivate a deeper connection with your audience. Each email becomes a building block in a robust relationship with your subscribers, which, in turn, drives loyalty and business growth. This dynamic approach ensures that your email marketing efforts remain an integral and efficient part of your broader digital marketing strategy, constantly evolving with your business needs and market trends.

As we close this chapter on mastering email marketing, remember that each section builds upon the last, forming a comprehensive guide designed to elevate your email campaigns from simple communications to powerful tools for business growth. Looking ahead, the strategies and insights shared here pave the way for deeper dives into other facets of digital marketing, ensuring you're equipped to send better emails and integrate these efforts into a broader, more effective marketing strategy.

9

Staying Ahead of Digital Marketing Trends

In your world, time is a resource just as precious as your tools. Keeping up-to-date with the latest digital marketing trends doesn't mean you need to sacrifice hours you don't have. The trick is to streamline the influx of information, have a framework to assess the data, and create a plan for implementation in your own business.

9.1 Adapting Without Getting Overwhelmed

Opt for curated newsletters and industry blogs that do the heavy lifting for you. These resources sift through the noise and deliver the gold nuggets directly to your inbox or feed. For instance, subscribing to a digital marketing newsletter like 'Marketing Dive' can provide you with a daily brief on what's new and noteworthy without you having to scour the internet. Join industry-specific mastermind groups on

LinkedIn or Facebook and check in periodically. This way, you stay informed with minimal time investment, keeping your focus sharp on running your business while still fostering growth through informed marketing strategies.

Not every shiny new trend will fit the unique needs of your local brick-and-mortar business. The evaluation of which trends to pursue should be as meticulous as selecting the right material for a crucial job. However, this process is not as daunting as it may seem. Begin by asking how a particular trend can enhance your customer interactions or streamline operations. Use a simple criterion: Does it add value? Will it connect more deeply with my customer base? Is it cost-effective? Answering these questions can help you filter out the fads from the truly beneficial innovations, giving you confidence in your decision-making. I will warn you that most entrepreneurs will find a way to add in some shiny new trend before they've mastered the basics, so remember, "fancy fails and simple scales."

If a trend does pass your initial evaluation, test it through small-scale pilot projects. This approach minimizes risk and allows for practical insights into whether a trend is worth a larger investment. Say you want to explore the effectiveness of video marketing. Instead of overhauling your marketing strategy, start by creating a series of short videos highlighting your work process or showcasing customer testimonials.

Monitor engagement and customer feedback. This pilot project can reveal whether videos might be worth integrating more fully into your marketing efforts or if they don't resonate with your audience as expected.

Lastly, there's immense value in learning from the landscape around you. Engage with peer networks or explore case studies of businesses similar to yours that have adopted new marketing trends. Observing the successes and failures of others can provide a roadmap and highlight potential pitfalls. For instance, if a local bakery gained substantial traction by integrating Instagram shopping into its strategy, consider how a similar approach could be tailored to your business. Online forums, webinars, and local business workshops are excellent venues for exchanging insights and experiences. By learning from the community, you can make informed decisions that align with both current trends and your business's authentic voice.

9.2 The Future of Digital Marketing for Local Small Businesses

Predictions about the future of digital marketing highlight a landscape that is perpetually evolving, with innovations that could transform how you connect with your customers and manage your online presence. As a small business owner, understanding these changes and preparing for them can seem daunting, but it's much like anticipating changes in the weather and adjusting your sails accordingly to maintain your course. For instance, the increasing integration of AI and machine learning into digital marketing tools is not just a trend for the big players; it's becoming accessible for small businesses too, offering you sophisticated tools that were once out of reach due to cost and complexity.

The role of AI in digital marketing is growing more significant by the day. AI algorithms can analyze customer data much more efficiently than a human ever could, identifying patterns and predicting customer behaviors with remarkable accuracy. For your small business, this might mean an AI-driven tool that personalizes product recommendations to each visitor on your website, potentially increasing sales. Or, think of AI-powered chatbots that can handle customer inquiries on your site 24/7, ensuring that you never miss an opportunity to engage with potential customers, even when you're busy on the job or after hours. These tools are designed to integrate seamlessly into your existing digital platforms, enhancing your capabilities without the need to expand your team.

As consumer expectations shift, particularly towards more personalized and immersive online experiences, your small business must adapt to stay competitive. Customers today expect a level of personalization that makes them feel understood and valued, not just another number in your sales figures. This could be as simple as personalized email marketing campaigns that address customers by name and recommend products based on previous purchases. Also, as privacy concerns grow, ensuring that your digital marketing strategies respect customer data and comply with privacy laws will become not just good practice but a necessity. This balance between personalization and privacy is delicate but essential, and positioning your business as one that customers can trust while providing them with a tailored experience can significantly boost customer loyalty and satisfaction.

Additionally, sustainability and ethical marketing are becoming more than just buzzwords; they are powerful trends shaping consumer preferences. A growing segment of consumers prefers to do business with brands that demonstrate social responsibility. For your local brick-and-mortar business, this might mean highlighting your sustainable practices, whether that's using local materials, supporting local community projects, or minimizing waste. Showing your business's commitment to ethical practices can be a significant differentiator, particularly as consumers become more conscientious about where they spend their money. Effectively marketing these efforts positions your brand as an ethical choice and can drive a deeper connection with your community and customer base.

As you navigate these developments, the key is to view them not as hurdles but as opportunities to enhance your business's appeal and operational efficiency. By staying informed and agile, willing to adopt new practices that align with your business values and customer expectations, you ensure your small business survives and thrives in the future digital marketing landscape. Adopting these forward-thinking strategies will help you maintain a competitive edge, making your business a preferred choice for customers who value personalization, privacy, sustainability, and ethical practices.

10

Conclusion

As we wrap up this journey through the world of digital marketing, it's important to reflect on what we've covered together. I know you're a small business owner with big dreams and real constraints, so it was important for me to give you straightforward, actionable, and practical advice that transcends theoretical fluff.

Throughout these pages, we've delved into the essentials of digital marketing—a critical arena for any small business looking to thrive in today's competitive environment. We started by setting a strong foundation, helping you understand the digital marketing landscape along with your own clarity and purpose. From there, we navigated through the intricacies of content and social media marketing, explored the tactical uses of paid online advertising and SEO, and demonstrated how to leverage email marketing for substantial growth. Each chapter was constructed to not only guide you but to equip you with the tools, templates, and checklists necessary to put your learning into action.

But remember, the heartbeat of this book has always been its actionable nature. It's not just about what digital marketing is but how you can use it to drive real results. By now, you should feel prepared to roll up your sleeves and dive into creating and implementing your digital marketing strategy, one that is tailored to your business's unique needs and aspirations.

However, the landscape of digital marketing is ever-evolving, and staying adaptable is crucial. I encourage you to maintain a mindset of continuous learning and curiosity. The world of online marketing will continue to change, and your ability to adapt will be key to your ongoing success.

Now, let's talk action. I urge you to take that first step, no matter how small, towards implementing the strategies we've discussed. Whether it's setting up your Google My Business listing, crafting your first social media post, or sending out an email campaign, remember that every journey begins with a single step. And each step you take is a move towards mastery and success in your business.

I'd like to thank you sincerely for investing your time in this book. Your commitment to growing your business is commendable, and I am grateful to be a part of your journey. As you apply the strategies outlined here, I encourage you to track your progress through analytics and continuously refine your approach based on real data and feedback.

Let's keep the conversation going. I am eager to hear about your successes and how you've applied what you've learned here to achieve real results. This book is just the beginning of your journey to digital marketing mastery, and I am excited to see where you go from here. Remember, in the world of small business, every big success starts with a dream and a willingness to take that first, bold step. Go make it happen.

Thank you once again, and here's to your success!

Time To Celebrate Your Success & Inspire Others

Your Review Can Lead To Another Turning Their Dream Into A Reality

> "Success is no accident. It is hard work, perseverance, learning, studying, sacrifice, and most of all, love of what you are doing." - Pelé

Congratulations! You've reached the end of *The Busy Entrepreneur's Guide To Digital Marketing*, and that's no small feat. You've taken the time to invest in your business, and now you're ready to see the rewards of your hard work.

But before you dive into your next big success, there's one more way you can make a difference.

By sharing your thoughts about this book, you can help other small business owners who are just like you—ready to take on the challenges of digital marketing but needing that final push to get started.

Your review could inspire someone else to achieve what you've just accomplished. Imagine being the reason another entrepreneur finds the courage to pursue their dreams and see them become reality. Think about how your experience could help...

...one more small business break through the noise...one more entrepreneur overcome their fears...one more family find financial security...one more customer discover a product or service that changes their life...one more dream come to life, just like yours.

Your review might seem like a small gesture, but it has the power to impact countless others who are looking to follow in your footsteps.

To share your experience, simply scan the QR code below and leave a review:

Thank you for being part of this journey and for helping others find their own path to success. Your story could be the spark that lights the way for someone else.

With deep appreciation,

Janessa Rhoades, Owner of Rhoades Consulting Group

References

Cox, L. K. (2024, July 2). 33 great landing page examples you'll want to copy in 2024. HubSpot. https://blog.hubspot.com/marketing/fantastic-landing-page-examples

McCormick, K. (2020, June 3). 13 Google My Business optimizations to rank higher in local search. WordStream. https://www.wordstream.com/blog/ws/2020/06/03/google-my-business-optimization

Patel, N. (n.d.). Local SEO keyword research (step-by-step guide). Neil Patel. https://neilpatel.com/blog/local-keyword-research/

Dean, B. (2024). Link building strategies: The complete list (2024). Backlinko. https://backlinko.com/link-building-strategies

HawkSEM. (n.d.). PPC for small business: 8 tips to drive more revenue. https://hawksem.com/blog/ppc-for-small-business/

How to Measure the ROI of Digital Marketing for a Small ... https://www.buzzboard.ai/how-to-measure-the-roi-of-digi

tal-marketing-for-a-small-business/#:~:text=To%20calcula te%20this%2C%20subtract%20the,other%20investments %20or%20business%20opportunities.

Small Business Marketing In 2024: The Ultimate Guide. (n.d.). Forbes. https://www.forbes.com/advisor/business/small-business-marketing/

How to Improve Your Local Business's Google Visibility - WebFX. (n.d.). WebFX. https://www.webfx.com/local-seo/learn/google-local-business/

Good, Better, Best: Creating Buyer Personas at Every Budget. (n.d.). The Mx Group. https://www.themxgroup.com/resources/how-to-create-buyer-personas-at-every-budget/

Digital Marketing ROI: Definition, Metrics, & How to Measure. (n.d.). WebFX. https://www.webfx.com/digital-marketing/learn/how-to-measure-digital-roi/

Bahene Tumwekwasize. (2023). The 6 Best Social Media Platforms for Your Business in 2023. LinkedIn. https://www.linkedin.com/pulse/6-best-social-media-platforms-your-business-2023-bahene-tumwekwasize

How to Completely Optimize Your GBP Listing. (n.d.). Search Engine Journal. https://www.searchenginejournal.com/local-seo/optimize-google-my-business/

30 Low-Cost Content Marketing Ideas. (n.d.). Writtent. https://writtent.com/blog/30-low-cost-ideas-for-content-marketing-on-a-shoestring-budget/

Top Social Media Statistics And Trends Of 2024. (n.d.). Forbes. https://www.forbes.com/advisor/business/social-media-statistics/

How to Create a Social Media Calendar and Stay Organized. (n.d.). Hootsuite. https://blog.hootsuite.com/how-to-create-a-social-media-content-calendar/

6 Free Social Media Management Tools to Make Life Easier. (n.d.). Duct Tape Marketing. https://ducttapemarketing.com/free-social-media-management-tools/

A Guide to Social Media Analytics for Small Businesses | CO. (n.d.). U.S. Chamber of Commerce. https://www.uschamber.com/co/grow/marketing/small-business-social-media-analytics-guide

Small business SEO and local search: the ultimate guide. (n.d.). Yoast. https://yoast.com/ultimate-guide-to-small-business-seo/

How to Set Up Google Display Ads - Complete Guide. (n.d.). MeasureSchool. https://measureschool.com/how-to-set-up-google-display-ads/

The Ultimate Guide to Social Media Marketing for Local Businesses. (n.d.). Neil Patel. https://neilpatel.com/blog/the-ultimate-guide-to-social-media-marketing-for-local-businesses/

Chen, J. (2022, August 19). How to Calculate the Return on Investment (ROI) of a Marketing Campaign. Investopedia. https://www.investopedia.com/articles/personal-finance/053015/how-calculate-roi-marketing-campaign.asp

20 Tips to Write Catchy Email Subject Lines [+ Examples]. (n.d.). HubSpot. https://blog.hubspot.com/marketing/improve-your-email-subject-line

50 Email Segmentation Strategies You Need To Use in 2024. (n.d.). OptinMonster. https://optinmonster.com/50-smart-ways-to-segment-your-email-list/

The Best Email Marketing Software for 2024. (n.d.). PCMag. https://www.pcmag.com/picks/the-best-email-marketing-software

17 Email Marketing Metrics Every Marketer Needs to Know. (n.d.). Campaign Monitor. https://www.campaignmonitor.com/blog/email-marketing/17-email-marketing-metrics-every-email-marketer-needs-to-know/

Content Marketing for Small Businesses: 9 Essential Tips. (n.d.). SEMrush. https://www.semrush.com/blog/content-marketing-for-small-businesses/

How to create a successful SEO content strategy in 2023. (2022, October 24). The Drum. https://www.thedrum.com/news/2022/10/24/how-create-successful-seo-content-strategy-2023

10+ Essential Low-Cost Content Marketing Tools. (n.d.). Volume Nine. https://www.v9digital.com/insights/10-essential-low-cost-content-marketing-tools/

How to Measure Content Marketing ROI (The Right Way). (2022, December 20). WordStream. https://www.wordstream.com/blog/ws/2022/12/20/content-marketing-roi

7 Steps To Building An Online Community (With Examples). (n.d.). Thinkific. https://www.thinkific.com/blog/how-to-build-an-online-community/

How to Ask & Get Good Customer Reviews [+Examples]. (n.d.). HubSpot. https://blog.hubspot.com/service/get-customer-reviews

The Ultimate Guide to Personalized Email for Every Marketer. (n.d.). Campaign Monitor. https://www.campaignmonitor.com/resources/guides/personalized-email/

13 Customer Loyalty Program Ideas & Examples. (n.d.). Fit Small Business. https://fitsmallbusiness.com/customer-loyalty-program-ideas/

McKinsey Report: Digital Marketing Trends for 2023. (n.d.). Signals. https://getsignals.ai/blog/mckinsey-report-digital-marketing-trends-for-2023/

9 Successful Digital Marketing Case Studies That Boosted. (n.d.). Single Grain. https://www.singlegrain.com/digital-marketing/9-successful-digital-marketing-case-studies/

Spot the Big Difference Between Trends and Fads in Marketing. (n.d.). JO Agency. https://joagency.com/blog/trends-and-fads-in-marketing/#:~:text=Often%20used%20interchangeably%2C%20the%20two,and%20fall%20just%20as%20fast.

Data-Driven Marketing: A Guide For Today's SMBs | Act! (n.d.). Act!. https://www.act.com/data-driven-marketing-a-guide-for-small-businesses/

Google Analytics For Small Business: A Step-by-Step Guide. (n.d.). Web.com. https://www.web.com/blog/how-to-use-google-analytics-for-small-business/

How to Leverage Data to Make Better Marketing Decisions. (n.d.). Improvado. https://improvado.io/blog/data-driven-marketing-decisions

The 15 Best A/B Testing Tools That Are Guaranteed to. (n.d.). Neil Patel. https://neilpatel.com/blog/a-b-testing-tools/

Google Analytics For Small Business: A Step-by-Step Guide. (n.d.). Web.com. https://www.web.com/blog/how-to-use-google-analytics-for-small-business/

Email marketing benchmarks & industry statistics. Mailchimp. (n.d.). https://mailchimp.com/resources/email-marketing-benchmarks/?igaag=154664726859&igaat=&igacm=20637339549&igacr=687230856184&igakw=&igamt=&igant=g&ds_c=DEPT_AOC_Google_Search_US_EN_NB_Acquire_Broad_DSA-Rsrc_US&ds_kids=p78250621731&ds_a_lid=dsa-2227026702184&ds_cid=71700000115207178&ds_agid=58700008574686663&gad_source=1&gclid=CjwKCAjwhvi0BhA4EiwAX25uj4rjgE63N35Vaswk5HGlC2eWBYdSxZU3Lfc24i45aAZQmuQxnKYDJhoCvqUQAvD_BwE&gclsrc=aw.ds

Campaign Monitor. (2022, March 10). What are good open rates, CTRs, & CTORs for email campaigns? https://www.campaignmonitor.com/resources/knowledge-base/what-are-good-email-metrics/#:~:text=What%20is%20the%20average%20click,average%20between%203%2D5%25.

Ammar-Mazhar. (2024, May 28). Email open rate: Statistics & 17 best practices (2024 guide). Mailmunch. https://www.mailmunch.com/blog/email-open-rate#:~:text=Email%20open%20rates%20are%20important,the%20sender%2C%20and%20the%20content.

Trafft. (n.d.). Services landing page: How to create the ultimate page to boost your bookings. https://trafft.com/services-landing-page/

ConvertFlow. (n.d.). Dental landing pages: How to create high-converting campaigns. https://www.convertflow.com/campaigns/dental-landing-pages

Made in the USA
Las Vegas, NV
16 March 2025